The Little Book of Danish Design
for Children and Curious Grown-Ups

The Li

of Dan

Marie Hugsted
with illustrations by Kitt Stuart Schwenn

tle Book
sh Design

for Children and
Curious Grown-Ups

Strandberg Publishing

Contents

A little introduction

Design is everywhere. It is the cup you drink from, the table you sit at, your clothes and your mobile phone; it is text, books, doorknobs, cutlery and many, many other things. Often we do not think about the fact that the things we use were designed by someone or why something looks exactly the way it does. But many people have done their very best to make good, functional things that make our everyday life both simpler and nicer.

The book you are holding in your hands is the result of my own curiosity. When I see a chair, a coffeepot or a lamp, I wonder ... What is it made of? What does it feel like to touch? Why is it put together the way it is? And what was the designer thinking while he or she created it?

There are already many thick books on design that will answer most of these kinds of questions. But they are all written for grown-ups – and I thought that was a shame because design holds so many fun stories and intriguing questions that are also interesting for children. That is why I wrote this book, which is easier to understand and probably also a little more fun. Maybe you can read the book yourself, but it can also be nice to have a grown-up read it to you.

Denmark has become world-famous for its strong design tradition, which is based on keeping things functional and simple. When you read the book, you will soon discover that many of the things we call design classics today were created because designers felt like experimenting with new materials and techniques.

The Danish lighting designer Poul Henningsen loved playing and taking chances, because he thought that the most interesting things happened when people played, explored or dared to try something new. You probably know from your own experience that when you explore and experiment, things sometimes go wrong – and that is not necessarily a bad thing. In fact, many mistakes have turned out to be the beginning of a new design. In this book, you can read about how designers work and how they come up with good ideas and test them to see how they function in practice. You can also learn about different materials and techniques, and you will discover that much of Danish design is driven by a passion for good craftsmanship.

The book looks at 50 different design objects that we use at home and which were created during the past 100 years or so. You probably know many of them already, but there will also be some you have never heard about. I have tried to include as many different things as possible in terms of both materials and functions – but as you will see, there are many chairs. That is because over the years, many Danish designers have focused in particular on making good chairs.

The book tells the story behind many of the things we know and live with every day and tries to help you see them from a new and different angle. That is also why it is illustrated with drawings instead of photos, unlike most design books, because drawings can help us see things in new ways.

Every time we choose to include something, we also choose to leave something out. In case there is a particular design object that you think is missing, there are some blank pages at the end of the book where you can make your own drawing. Maybe you have a favourite object that deserves to be included in the book?

In addition to the 50 stories about design objects, the book has four short chapters about important design themes that can help you understand what design is about and why it is important for us to be surrounded by good design.

You can read the book from cover to cover, or you can use it to look things up, as a basis for talking about design with others or as inspiration to explore some of the design objects you know from your own everyday life. I hope that it will make you want to go out to look at design – for example, at a museum or in a shop. You can examine how things are put together, what they are made of and whether you think they work as intended. At the back of the book is a glossary that explains key design terms and concepts. In the text, the words that are included in the glossary are written in blue.

The original Danish version of this book was made possible by generous support from the following private foundations: Nikolai og Felix Fonden, the New Carlsberg Foundation, Beckett-Fonden and Politiken-Fonden. I am grateful to my editor, Sidsel Kjærulff Rasmussen, and my design consultant, Pernille Stockmarr, for good, rewarding and constructive talks and support. I also thank Anne-Louise Sommer, director of Designmuseum Danmark, for supporting the project from day one. I thank Søren Damstedt, who created the graphic design of the book, and all the designers and companies that helped me with information. Many thanks also to Dorte H. Silver for the very competent translation and to proofreader Wendy Brouwer for adding the important finishing touches to the text. Finally, warm thanks go to illustrator Kitt Stuart Schwenn for the wonderful drawings.

Marie Hugsted

Light and shade

We begin our story of Danish design in light of a great designer.

Many think that lampshades are only about decoration, but they serve an important function in addition to looking nice: diffusing the light and preventing glare by shielding the bright electric bulb so it does not dazzle the eye. One of the first people to be interested in this was the brilliant Danish designer Poul Henningsen. Most people called him by his initials, PH, and that is also the name he used for his lamps.

A hundred years ago, most homes in Denmark were lit by paraffin lamps, which have a warm, soft light. Around 1920, many Danish homes had electricity installed and began to use lamps with electric light bulbs, which have a sharper, colder light. In the beginning, people used old-fashioned lampshades made of cloth, but they made the light very dim, and many of them did not shield the light bulb properly. They were also unsafe, because they might catch fire if the bulb got too hot.

PH was known as a cheerful man, but he had zero patience with glare or dazzling light. His dream was to design a lampshade that would direct the light to where it was needed, not just into the room or up into the ceiling, as many lamps did at the time. He also wanted to cover up the light bulb because he did not think it looked nice.

He made hundreds of experiments with a set of shades that looked like a dinner plate, a soup plate and a cup, which he stacked in different ways. In the right configuration, the shades gave a pleasant light and kept the dazzling light from hitting the eye directly and producing glare.

PH also experimented with lampshades in different colours in order to give the light the right tone. This made his lamps stand out as very different from any other lamps people could buy at the time. The first PH-lamp was designed in 1926 for a car show in Copenhagen. It took 30 years before the PH-lamps had their real breakthrough with the PH 5 model, which is now in use in more than 300,000 Danish homes!

Although PH is no longer alive, his lamps live on, as do his ideas about exploring and creating the right light. It seems safe to say he had some really bright ideas.

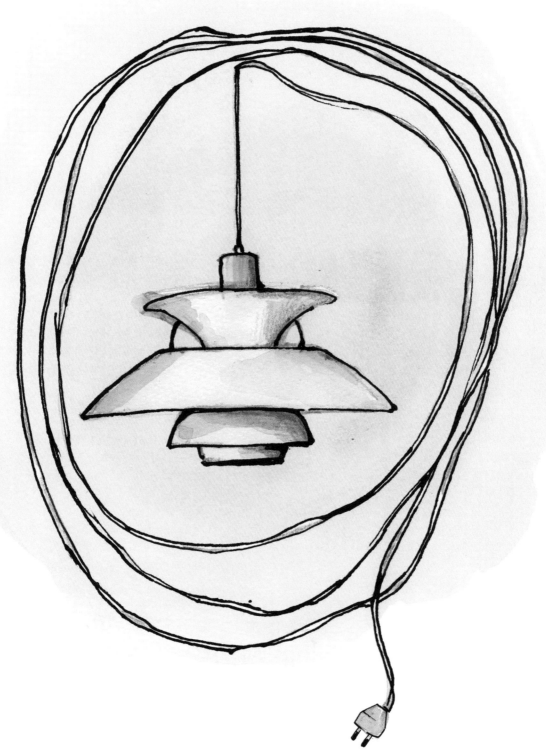

Milk carton ·
Carl Hartmann, 1929

Milk in bottles,
bags and boxes

Has it ever occurred to you that all the boxes, wrappers, cartons, bags and so forth that food and other things come in were designed by someone? They are all examples of packaging design. Every time a product leaves a factory, someone first had to figure out what the packaging should look like: choosing a shape, materials, colours and writing that fit the product and keep it fresh and safe. Packaging has to be practical and functional, and it has to show what the content is and make you want to buy the product. That is also the case for the milk carton.

A milk carton has several jobs to do. First, it has to store the milk safely, and be easy to open and close again, so the milk does not go off. Second, it should be practical to handle and transport: this means it has to have a form that is easy to stack and which fits into the crates that are used to transport the cartons from the factory to the supermarket refrigerator. And third, it has to have a design that stands out from other milk cartons and which can be used to provide important information about the product so you know what is inside.

In the past, milk came in glass bottles and was delivered straight to your doorstep by the milkman. This was back when most people did not have a refrigerator in the home. Families ordered the milk they needed for the day and had to remember to drink it right away or it would go off. The milkman picked up the empty glass bottles and returned them to the plant where they were cleaned and reused.

In 1929, Carl Hartmann designed a milk container made of heavy paper with a waterproof lining. He called it a milk bag and patented his invention. It was practical, lightweight and sturdy and offered a convenient alternative to the milk bottle.

Carl Hartmann's milk bags are not very different from the milk cartons we use today. Since then, the milk carton has been developed further by the American company Pure Pak, which added the tall gable that makes the carton look like a house. Many have tried to design a new and better milk carton using different shapes and materials, but as consumers we prefer the carton we are familiar with. There has only been one important addition since then – the plastic cap, which was added in 2008 to make it possible to store the milk carton lying down, even after it has been opened.

An old proverb says we should not cry over spilled milk. Without proper packaging, we would surely have a lot of good milk going to waste!

Bin it!

Back in 1939, the young hairdresser Marie Axelsen was about to open her own salon in the city of Randers in northern Jutland, and she needed a practical bin. She wanted a bin with a lid that she could open even when she had her hands full. She also wanted the bin to be sturdy and look nice. She mentioned this to her husband, Holger Nielsen, who set to work designing a bin that was exactly the way she wanted it.

Holger Nielsen was inspired by American pedal bins, which can be operated hands-free because the lid flips up when you step on a pedal. After many attempts, Holger Nielsen designed a simple, cylindrical metal bin with a lid that flips up. He called it Vipp, based on the Danish word for 'flip'. He added handles to the sides to make it easy to move around and a large base to make it stable so it would not get knocked over by accident.

Marie Axelsen loved her Vipp bin and used it every day in her salon. Although Holger Nielsen had no plans of making additional bins, he soon received requests for bins from doctors and dentists who also saw the benefits of the sturdy and hygienic pedal bin.

Holger Nielsen was not much of a businessman, so the Vipp bin was not produced in large numbers while he was alive. But his daughter Jette thought that more people should be able to enjoy her dad's invention. In 1992, she took over production, and since then things have moved fast. The bin is now found in many Danish homes and is sold in more than 30 countries around the world.

The Vipp bin has been called 'the world's most expensive waste bin', and, indeed, it is far from cheap. Maybe you think it is silly to pay so much for a waste bin when you could simply use a bag instead. But the bin is really useful, also in a private home. It can hold a big bag, and the tight-fitting lid keeps any nasty smells inside. Many people also like it because it looks nice, like a neat piece of furniture. Today, the Vipp bin is more popular than ever and a good example that a design that was developed for a very specific purpose can be used in a much wider range of contexts.

Growing pains

Sometimes, a tragic story can provide the inspiration for a new design. That was certainly the case when the Juno cot bed was created.

On a summer's day in 1942, architect Viggo Einfeldt was reading his morning newspaper, as he did every day. In the paper, he read about a child who had got his head stuck in between the bars of his cot and had tragically died – any parent's worst nightmare. The article made Viggo Einfeldt very upset and gave him the idea to design a cosy cot bed where the child would be safe and sound.

At the time, safety was not a top priority in the design of cots and beds. Viggo Einfeldt changed that. In addition to worrying about safety, he also wanted to make a practical bed. Therefore, he made it adjustable, so that it can grow as the child grows from baby to toddler to junior. Simply pull out the bed and it extends. When the Juno bed was first presented, it was under the slogan 'The bed that grows with your child'.

In case you are wondering why the bed is called Juno, the name was chosen by Viggo Einfeldt's daughter. She discovered that Juno was name of a Roman goddess who was said to watch over women while they are giving birth. That makes it a perfect name for the bed.

Although the design of the Juno bed was inspired by a tragic event, the second part of the story has a happy ending. Designers began to focus more on keeping children safe, and many children enjoyed having a bed that grew longer as they grew taller. The bed proved so popular that it is now being produced again. It is amazing to think that the same design has lasted so long. In fact, many of the beds that were made more than 60 years ago were passed down from generation to generation and are still in use today.

Viggo Einfeldt followed his dream – and created a bed where lots of children have had many happy dreams. What is your dream?

Big design for small people

Design for children

Since you were little, you have been surrounded by things that were specially designed for you and other children. Everything, from cups and beds to chairs and clothes, is created with children in mind. It is designed to be the right size for a child and to be sturdy and safe so that it makes everyday life easier – for children as well as their parents.

Denmark and the other Nordic countries have a strong tradition for knowing and understanding children's needs and are some of the world's leading countries when it comes to creating design for children. Scissors, furniture, prams, playgrounds and thousands of other things are designed for children and make it both safer and more fun to be a little kid in a big world.

It was not always like that. Over the past century, there has been a big shift in what it is like to be a child in Denmark.

Children began to be viewed as an independent group, not just as miniature adults who need to adapt to the world they were born into.

Adults have also become more aware of how best to give children a safe and good childhood. That is why the 20th century is often called 'the century of the child'.

Along with these changes in society, designers have also begun to take an interest in how they can adapt everyday settings and objects to children's needs.

Some things made for children are items you might not think about as design. In 2010, the Danish company Novo Nordisk presented a special injection pen that makes it safer and simpler for children with diabetes to take their medicine without needing help from a grown-up. That means that they do not need to worry so much about their diabetes, and it makes easier for them to play with other children on equal terms.

In 2012, the Danish-Icelandic artist Olafur Eliasson designed the lamp called Little Sun, which is powered by solar energy. The lamp was made for the millions of children in poor countries who do not have access to electricity and who cannot do their homework after the sun has set. If you leave the lamp out in the sun during the day, it is charged by solar energy, so that you can switch it on when it gets dark. Designers make many things that improve life for children all over the world.

The bicycle is an example of how it makes sense to design products specially for children. In Denmark, many people ride a bicycle every day, and most children learn to ride a bicycle from an early age. The scooter is a brilliant invention for toddlers who are too young to be able to

balance on a normal bicycle but want to practice to get ready for a proper two-wheeler.

In 2016, Danish schools introduced the new school subject Craft and Design, because in Denmark we think it is important for children to learn about design, materials and crafts and to get inspiration for new inventions. Children are often more curious, experimental and playful in their approach to the world than adults, so it makes good sense to encourage children to create tomorrow's designs.

Maybe you already have a good idea for something you could design?

A chair that is a toy that is a chair

Peter's chair is an example of how a shortage of materials can inspire designers to be inventive and come up with new solutions.

In 1944, the furniture designer Hans J. Wegner was working on the interior of the new City Hall in Aarhus, a building that was designed by his colleague Arne Jacobsen. One summer's day, he was told that his good friend Børge Mogensen had had a son, who was going to be named Peter. So he went out to find a christening present for the little boy. As this was during the Second World War, there were many things people could not buy in the shops, and he could not find a proper present.

Instead, Wegner decided to make a present himself. He went into his workshop and made a small child-sized chair for the boy. He wanted to make a very special piece of furniture. It had to be both a chair and a toy. Therefore, he made the chair out of four parts that could be assembled without the use of screws or glue to form a stable seat. The idea was that as Peter grew older, he would be able to take apart and reassemble his own chair. The fact that it could be taken apart was also clever because it made it easy to pack it in a flat box and send by post to Copenhagen, where the christening was to take place. Finally, Wegner gave the chair rounded corners so Peter could not hurt himself on his chair.

Peter's dad, Børge Morgensen, was the director of a large furniture design office in Copenhagen called the FDB Design Office. When he saw the chair, he liked it so much that he decided to put it into production. He also asked Wegner to design a little child-sized table to go with the chair.

Peter's chair and Peter's table showed a whole new way of designing children's furniture. Before this time, furniture designers had not had much interest in children's furniture. Often, children's furniture was simply miniature versions of furniture for adults, and sometimes it was not in the best quality. By creating children's furniture that could also be used as a toy and was made in high-quality materials, Wegner created a new tradition, which came to shape furniture design for children for many years to come.

Handmade fruits

The story behind the Fruit lamp begins more than 100 years ago, when architect Peder Vilhelm Jensen-Klint needed a shade for his paraffin lamp and decided to design one himself. This was before people had electricity, so they used wax candles and paraffin lamps after dark.

Peder Vilhelm Jensen-Klint was inspired by the Chinese and Japanese art of paper folding, so he made a lampshade by pleating – another word for folding – a large sheet of heavy paper over and over again. Using this technique he created a simple and elegant shade that shielded the light. He was so pleased with the outcome that he made more shades, which he gave as gifts to his friends and family – and people liked them. As more and more people were interested in the lampshades, he had his sons, Tage and Kaare, help him pleat more shades after school. Over the years, the three men in the family designed many different models. What had begun as a family project eventually became big business.

The youngest son, Kaare Klint, trained as an architect. In his work, he was especially interested in spatial and geometric shapes. In 1944, he designed the Fruit lamp, which has become the most popular of the Klint shades. Kaare Klint was inspired by Chinese paper lamps, and because he had so many years' experience pleating paper, he was able to create a sophisticated three-dimensional ball-shaped shade with a complex pattern of many tiny folds called cross-pleats. As you can see, the Fruit lamp looks like a fruit – maybe an apple?

Many clever engineers have tried to invent machines that can fold the lampshades faster than a person can, but they have never been successful. The pleats are so complicated that only specially trained workers can make them, and it takes many years to learn the skill. That is why all the Klint lampshades are still folded by hand today. In fact, they are still folded on the island of Funen, close to where the family has lived for the past 100 years.

The Fruit lamp itself moved into the limelight in 1960 when it appeared in the film *Let's Make Love* with the American film star Marilyn Monroe. That made the lamp world-famous.

Spoke-Back sofa ·
Børge Mogensen, 1945

The sofa that spoke back

In 1945, an elegant and understated sofa
was presented at the Copenhagen
Cabinetmakers' Guild exhibition. The sofa
was designed by the young cabinetmaker
Børge Mogensen, who is still remembered
today as one of Denmark's greatest
furniture designers. Like many other
furniture designers at the time, Mogensen
was tired of the heavy, overstuffed furniture
that was popular at the time. He also
thought that soft, padded sofas were boring
and made people lazy. So he designed the
Spoke-Back sofa, which is light and airy,
looks harmonious from every angle and is
adapted to the proportions of the human
body. It has a slender and upright wooden
frame with spokes in the back and sides, and
cushions with a tight wool upholstery in
characteristic chequered patterns designed
by the weaver Lis Ahlmann. The inspiration
for the Spoke-Back sofa came from
furniture types from other countries: a
French chaise longue, which is a sort of sofa
with a backrest at one end, and the English
daybed, which is a couch people have in the
living room that can also be used as a bed.
Mogensen liked sofas that you could stretch
out on – that is why one of the sides of the
Spoke-Back sofa can be folded all the way
down.

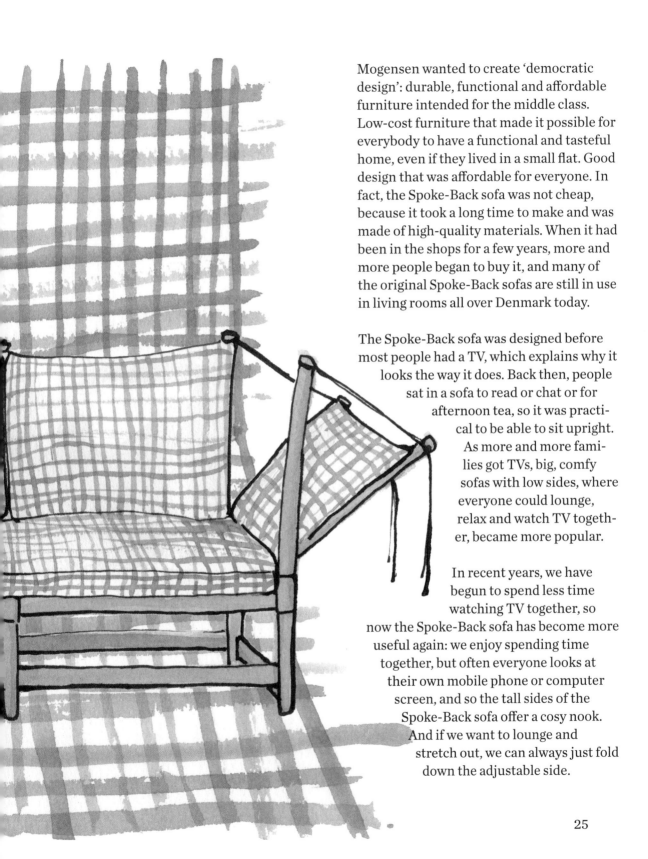

Mogensen wanted to create 'democratic design': durable, functional and affordable furniture intended for the middle class. Low-cost furniture that made it possible for everybody to have a functional and tasteful home, even if they lived in a small flat. Good design that was affordable for everyone. In fact, the Spoke-Back sofa was not cheap, because it took a long time to make and was made of high-quality materials. When it had been in the shops for a few years, more and more people began to buy it, and many of the original Spoke-Back sofas are still in use in living rooms all over Denmark today.

The Spoke-Back sofa was designed before most people had a TV, which explains why it looks the way it does. Back then, people sat in a sofa to read or chat or for afternoon tea, so it was practical to be able to sit upright. As more and more families got TVs, big, comfy sofas with low sides, where everyone could lounge, relax and watch TV together, became more popular.

In recent years, we have begun to spend less time watching TV together, so now the Spoke-Back sofa has become more useful again: we enjoy spending time together, but often everyone looks at their own mobile phone or computer screen, and so the tall sides of the Spoke-Back sofa offer a cosy nook. And if we want to lounge and stretch out, we can always just fold down the adjustable side.

Shark's Fin tin opener · Jens Quistgaard, 1950

A steel shark

Some things are so well designed we can hardly imagine them looking any other way. That's the case with the Shark's Fin, a tin opener designed by Jens Quistgaard. The Shark's Fin got its name both because it looks like a shark's fin and because it slices effortlessly through metal, like a shark's fin gliding through water.

Although the Shark's Fin looks simple, Quistgaard paid attention to every detail and left nothing to chance. It is a piece of bent steel with a sharp fin that is able to cut through tin. The flat piece has tiny grooves that give you a good grip, so your hand does not slip when you use it. Every single feature has a purpose, and in that way the Shark's Fin reflects what designers mean when they say that 'form follows function'. This means that the designer has removed all superfluous elements and gone to the functional core of the object. The goal is maximum simplicity, where every aspect of the form is determined by function.

In 1950, when the Shark's Fin was designed, tinned food was new and modern. If you needed a quick meal, it was easy to open a tin and heat up the contents. That has changed, and today most people do not think of tinned food as fancy. Today, many tins come with a ring pull, so eventually we may not need the Shark's Fin to get at our tinned delights.

Although few people in Denmark know the name Jens Quistgaard, thousands of Danish families have a Shark's Fin in their kitchen drawer without knowing that it is an important design icon. Quistgaard was the head of a design studio in the United States for many years, and in America he may be the best-known Danish designer – not for the Shark's Fin but for the Kobenstyle series of colourful kitchenware made of thin iron treated to look like enamel.

By the way, the tin opener was invented in 1858 – 48 years after the sealed tin. How people opened their tins until then is a good question!

Make a wish

Just as artists are often inspired by the work of other artists, designers are often inspired by the work of other designers. Hans J. Wegner loved visiting the Danish Museum of Art & Design, which is now called Design-museum Danmark, because it had the country's finest collection of chairs. Here he studied different chair types, examined their history and made precise drawings of them to under-stand how they had been constructed. These studies helped him learn about what makes a good chair and inspired him to design chairs himself.

The Wishbone chair is a good example of the way he worked. It also shows us how the objects that we think of as Danish designs have found inspiration in traditions from all over the world. Wegner took the best elements from several known chair types and used them as his starting point when he designed the Wishbone chair. The top rail, which is the rounded part of the backrest, was inspired by old Chinese chairs. The Y-shaped splat, which is the board that forms the backrest, was inspired by English Windsor chairs.

Wegner liked to explore how wood could be used. Dry wood is hard to bend, so he used a special technique called steam-bending. When wood is heated with steam it can be shaped and rounded. Steam-bending was used to make the so-called bentwood chairs created by the Thonet brothers in Austria, which had also inspired him. The woven seat was inspired by tradi-tional Greek peasant chairs.

Although the Wishbone chair has elements from several different chair types, it is not a copy of any other chair. Wegner simply built on experience from the history of chair design all over the world to create a variant that was of good quality and simpler to produce than earlier handmade chairs. Maybe that is why it seems timeless and has remained modern and popular.

Much of the Wishbone chair is still made by hand today. The seat is made of 80 metres of paper cord. It takes an experienced specialist an hour to weave.

If you have ever had chicken or turkey cooked whole, you can probably guess why it is called the Wishbone chair. The Y-shaped backrest looks just like the wishbone on a bird. Have you ever pulled a wishbone with someone to see who got to make a wish?

Monkey business

In 1951, a cheeky little monkey came into the world on a carpenter's workbench. The monkey was made by Kay Bojesen, and even though he had trained as a silversmith, he also loved making toys out of wood.

He had been asked to design a wall hook for clothes for an exhibition of children's furniture. Instead of designing an ordinary wall hook, he wanted to make something that would activate a child's imagination. The result was the lively monkey whose hands and feet were curved, so they could hold a jacket or a hat. As it turned out, the Monkey was more fun as a toy than as a wall hook, but the playful animal soon got a grip on its new job.

Since then, the Monkey with the charming underbite and bubbly personality has charmed both children and grown-ups. With its bright eyes and round belly, it almost looks a little like Bojesen himself. He had a warm and playful attitude and wanted the Monkey to make children happy and curious.

It may be hard to see, but the Monkey actually consists of 32 different parts. The body is made of dark teak, while the belly and face are made of the lighter limba wood. The exotic wood types seem a good choice for a monkey, who comes from the jungle, far away from Denmark. Still, the clear shapes and high quality reflect the key characteristics Danish design is known for.

Like other celebrities, the Monkey has travelled all over the world; it has been on TV and taken part in exhibitions in the finest museums. The most exciting experience the Monkey had was probably when Bojesen took it on a trip to the zoo so it could meet a real live chimpanzee.

Today most people know the Monkey as a decorative object that climbs bookcases or leaps from lamp cord to lamp cord in the living room. But ever since it first came out, it has also been used as a toy in preschools and private homes. Even though it is not soft, it feels nice to the touch, and it is fun to play with. The Monkey lives in many Danish homes, so if you meet one on your way, maybe you should ask it if it wants to play.

A hard-working ant

Arne Jacobsen was a productive man. He designed a whole range of famous chairs as well as many smaller things, such as watches, clocks, lamps, water taps and cutlery. He also designed houses, city halls, a petrol station and even a hotel and everything inside it.

The Ant is a good name for Jacobsen's chair from 1952. It was the first chair he designed, and originally it was called No. 3100. If you look at it, you can see that the narrow waist and skinny legs make it look like an ant, so that became the chair's nickname.

Jacobsen had been asked to design a chair for the canteen at a company called Novo Nordisk. He had been told to make the chair fairly small, lightweight, comfortable and stackable. He decided to cut to the bone and designed a chair that used as little material as possible. The result was the Ant, an unusual little chair made of only two elements: an undercarriage with three skinny steel legs and a thin shell made of moulded plywood that formed the seat and back. Jacobsen said that three legs was enough to make the chair stable, so the fourth leg was unnecessary.

As a designer, Jacobsen was curious to try out new techniques and materials. For the Ant, he used a new type of plywood that had been invented during the Second World War for making aeroplanes. Plywood is made of thin sheets of wood layered and glued in a criss-cross pattern. That makes the wood strong and flexible enough to be bent without cracking.

The unique thing about the Ant is the so-called double curvature of the plywood shell. Double curvature means that the wood is bent in two different curves to match the shape of the body. To make that possible, Jacobsen had to give the chair its characteristic narrow waist, which also gave him the inspiration for the name. The form was determined by what was technically possible when the wood was pushed to the max.

The Ant was the first chair in the world where the seat and back are made in a single piece. It was also the first mass-produced chair in Denmark. Mass production means making many identical items in a factory. This makes it possible to produce the chairs much faster than in the traditional approach, where a cabinetmaker makes everything by hand.

Your personal assistants

Form and function

Do you own something that works really well, and have you ever wondered why it is so useful? It is probably because it makes everyday life easier. Glasses make it easier to see, a good chair makes you comfortable when you want to relax, and good castors make it easy to move an office chair across the floor. We are surrounded by things intended to make our everyday life as good as possible because they are designed to serve a particular function.

Some of our things we hold on to because they have a history, because they look nice or because they have special meaning to us. Other things are important because they serve a purpose or because they help us handle practical everyday tasks.

We need to be able to open a door, hold a cup without burning our fingers and be comfortable when we sit. These are functions. That is why we need doorknobs, teacup handles and chairs.

Many designs have the purpose of connecting form and function, and there is a real art to combining the two. There is no point in making a tin opener that has a nice form if it cannot actually open a tin.

On the other hand, we should also like and enjoy the thing and be able to understand how to use it when we see it. If we look at lamps, for example, any light bulb can provide light, but the design of the lampshade affects how the light falls and whether we would want to have the lamp in our home.

More than 100 years ago, many craftspeople spent a great deal of time refining the things they made by decorating them with flourishes and intricate patterns. Decorative objects showed off the skill and effort the craftsperson had put into the task.

Many of the fine, handmade products from that period have been passed down from generation to generation because they are precious and rare.

In the 1930s, designers and architects from all over Europe began to be inspired by the new industrial production methods, which made it possible to make things faster and cheaper.

Many designers were fascinated by the new technology and experimented with how they could use it to make everyday life better and simpler. They were inspired by the look of new materials, such as steel and plastic, and also sought to simplify the shape of their products so they could be produced by machines.

The designers followed the motto of 'form follows function', which means that the purpose of the product decides the physical design. This movement and the style it represented was called functionalism, and ever since, many designers and architects have been inspired by functionalist ideals. Many of the designs shown in this book were created in accordance with the principles of functionalism – for example, the PH-lamp and the Ant chair.

When things are simple, it is particularly important that the designer does a good job. When a thing does not have any decoration or ornamentation, the form and the materials stand out more. We see this in Finn Juhl's Turning tray, for example, where Juhl has taken great care to design beautiful joints in the wood and to find materials that look good together.

Designers spend a lot of time on making things that function as intended. But even if we know what a thing was intended for, we might still use it for a different purpose.

Kay Bojesen's Monkey, for example, was originally designed as a wall hook for clothes, but today it is mostly used as a toy or as decoration. And the book you are holding right now can be used for many other things besides reading – for example, you can use it as a ping pong paddle, a fly-swatter, a fan, an umbrella or a dustpan. You can also use it to hit someone with or as a shield if someone attacks you – in fact, you can even tear out the pages to make paper aeroplanes or if you need to start a fire, although I sincerely hope you won't.

Margrethe bowl · Jacob Jensen, 1954

A royal bowl

You can find a Margrethe bowl in almost any kitchen cupboard in Denmark. From when the bowl was first launched until today, more than 50 million bowls have been produced.

Sigvard Bernadotte was a designer. He was also born as a prince in the Swedish royal family, and he was the uncle of a little Danish girl named Margrethe. He had a design studio in Copenhagen together with his friend Acton Bjørn.

In 1952, the design firm Bernadotte & Bjørn hired Jacob Jensen, who had just completed his training as a designer. One of his first assignments was to design a kitchen bowl for a company named Rosti. Back then, Rosti was a small company with a small budget, so Jensen was told not to spend too many hours on the task. Two days later, he presented his proposal, which was approved and put into production.

When the Margrethe bowl was launched onto the market, it was presented as 'a new kitchen item for the housewife'.

The material was a hard type of plastic called melamine, which does not absorb the colour or the flavour of the stuff that is poured into the bowl. This meant that you could use the bowl for mixing both turkey stuffing and cookie dough – but not at the same time!

The bowl was lightweight, sturdy and with a clever design: it had a handle you could hold on to while stirring and a little spout for pouring out the mix. This was very modern and novel.

If Jensen had known how successful the Margrethe bowl would be, he might have insisted on a different agreement with his boss. Instead, he just received his normal salary. If he had asked for just a small fee for every bowl that was sold, he could have retired young and never had to work again. Luckily for us, he did not, so ever since he has worked as a designer and developed many great products, including designs for Bang & Olufsen.

You probably already guessed whom the Margrethe bowl was named after: Bernadotte's niece. At the time, she was a little princess. Today she is the Queen of Denmark.

A flat-pack chair

Most of the furniture we have looked at in this book is made mainly of wood because Denmark has a proud tradition for high-quality handmade products in wood. Furniture designer Poul Kjærholm broke with that tradition when he designed the simple steel-frame easy chair called PK22.

As his graduation project from the School of Arts and Crafts in 1951, Kjærholm designed a chair that he called the PK25. It soon became very popular abroad, but because it could not be disassembled, delivery was quite expensive. The PK22 is a revised version of that. The two chairs are quite similar, but the PK22 has been improved because it can be disassembled and reassembled with just a few screws. When it is disassembled, it can be packed flat in a crate, which makes it easy to transport. That helped make the PK22 an international success. It was easy to ship all over the world – and with its straight lines and simple expression, it was a perfect example of the style that was popular during the 1950s.

The PK22 consists of a steel frame and a seat upholstered in leather, canvas or rattan. Rattan is the core from a climbing palm that looks a little like dried straw. The frame is assembled with black screws – a simple and practical choice.

The PK22 is a minimalistic easy chair, a type that is often called a 'lounge chair'. With its clean, straight lines, it moves away from the organic design that was modern during the 1950s, which is probably part of the reason why it became so successful. It is low, not particularly soft, and it does not have armrests – so it is not because it is supremely comfortable that it has become so popular. It is because it looks so elegant.

The funny thing is that even though the PK22 was Kjærholm's most famous chair, he never owned one himself.

Self-blown

Have you ever made a drawing and accidentally made a mistake? Instead of throwing the drawing away, it might be fun to see if the mistake can be used to make something new. In the mistake, something unexpected might happen, something unforeseen. When we are open to the possibilities that a mistake might hold, new things can happen. The glass-blower Per Lütken knew this when he accidentally created a glass bowl, in 1955, that he could not have imagined or drawn.

His idea was to shape the hot molten glass over a wooden form to create a beautiful, perfectly round bowl. Glass is a fragile material that can be difficult to handle. When it is shaped, it is heated to over 1,000 degrees Celsius. That makes it soft and malleable. Remember that boiling water is 'only' 100 degrees Celsius. Because the glass is so hot, a cloud of steam occurs if it comes into contact with something damp.

Lütken's mistake was that he had forgotten to make air holes in the damp wooden form to let the steam escape. As a result, there was a tiny explosion when the hot molten glass hit the wooden form. 'Poof!' it went. The pressure of the steam inflated the glass instead of shaping it into a bowl. The result looked like a soap bubble cut in half. It looked nothing like the neat bowl shape Lütken had imagined. Still, he saw a potential in the bowl, which went on to become one of the most famous glass bowls ever made in Denmark.

Because the bowl had been created in such an unusual way, the process is difficult to copy, and only the best glass-blowers can make the bowl today. It is much too complicated to make on a machine.

Originally, the bowl was named the Arne bowl, after Arne Boas, who was the director of the Holmegaard glassworks, where Lütken worked, and who had originally hired Lütken as a glass-blower. After a few years, the glassworks stopped making and selling the bowl because it was not popular enough with the customers.

In 1983, it was relaunched under the more poetic name the Provence bowl. Provence is an area in France that is known for good food and wine and for its unique and beautiful light. The name was picked more or less by chance, but at Holmegaard they felt that the new name suited the bowl. Whether it is the new name that has made the bowl more popular is hard to determine.

Two sides of the same tray

As we have seen, material shortages can lead to new designs. So can an excess of materials. During the 1950s, the production of Danish designs in teak went up. This was because a vast number of teak trees had been cut down in the Philippines during the Second World War to clear space for new roads for the military. Denmark was able to buy the timber cheaply after the war, and many designers seized the opportunity.

Finn Juhl was one of Denmark's most important designers during that period, which is known as the post-war period and is also called the golden age of Danish design. Juhl loved teak, and in 1956 he created the simple and elegant Turning tray. As the name suggests, the tray can be turned around. One side is black, while the other has one of the colours that were trendy when the tray came out: light blue, mint green, white or bright red. So on any given day, you can choose which side to use, depending on your mood.

The Turning tray has a teak frame and a laminate surface. If you look carefully, you can see the quality of the craftsmanship. The frame is joined with a so-called finger joint where the wood is cut and put together in a way that looks like fingers interlaced. The frame has a curve right where you grip it, which makes the tray easier to pick up and carry. Juhl paid great attention to details and became famous – both in Denmark and around the world – for his sense of quality and good craftsmanship.

The Turning tray is still handmade in Denmark. It is a beautiful design and an example that Danish designers were not only interested in making furniture. They also wanted to create other good and functional things for everyday use, like a tray, for example. Juhl had a dream of finding the time to design every single object in his own home: chairs, tables, rugs, wallpaper, curtains, plates, glasses, lamps and vases. Today, his house is a public museum. If you visit, you can see just how many things he did manage to design.

A chair made of spindles

Thirteen spindles, a top rail and a seat – that is all it takes to make a chair. Poul M. Volther liked to keep things simple. He had trained as a cabinetmaker and then went to the School of Arts and Crafts to become a furniture designer, so he was both a skilled craftsman and a designer. His style is known as Scandinavian functionalism, because he aimed for a functional and simple look based on quality materials and good craftsmanship. This is reflected in the popular chair J46, which is also known as the Spindle-Back chair.

The Spindle-Back chair is a kitchen chair made of beechwood and was part of a furniture series that the company FDB put into production from the design studio it founded in 1942. FDB wanted to change the way the Danes decorated their homes. At this time, just after the Second World War, most Danish homes were decorated with heavy and impractical tables, chairs and sofas. The designers in the FDB studio wanted to offer people better furniture – furniture that was simple and modern, made of wood and created by talented furniture designers. It was a democratic project with a philosophy of creating good, simple furniture that people could

afford. At the time, people often invested large amounts of money in furniture – on the other hand, they rarely needed to replace it because the furniture they bought would last a lifetime. This was before the first IKEA store came to Denmark and introduced the idea of cheap, mass-produced furniture.

Volther became the director of the FDB design studio in 1950 and put a wide range of chairs, easy chairs and sofas into production. In addition to managing the studio, he also created his own designs. He liked a simple and minimalist style, and like the Spindle-Back chair his furniture had a clean, discreet look. The Spindle-Back chair is functional and humble and does not call attention to itself. That may be why it is so popular in Denmark. In 2013, FDB put the chair back into production, and it has become very successful: by now, more than a million Spindle-Back chairs have been sold – that is close to one for every five people in Denmark.

Cutting-edge cutlery

Imagine you were going to design a set of cutlery for the future. That might be what Arne Jacobsen was thinking when he designed the AJ cutlery.

At first glance, the cutlery pieces look like surgical instruments. The simple shapes and the smooth transition between the handle and the blade of the knife, the tines of the fork or the bowl of the spoon do not make you think of potatoes and gravy. Again, Jacobsen was ahead of his time, and in this case he might have focused more on form than on function. The cutlery is tricky to eat with because the parts are so delicate – also, the tines on the fork are quite short, and the blade of the knife is not very sharp.

The AJ cutlery was part of Jacobsen's grand project of designing the SAS Royal Hotel in Copenhagen. He had been asked to design the entire hotel, top to bottom: the building, the furniture and the lamps – everything, every last detail. The cutlery was meant to be used in the hotel restaurant, so that the guests could experience the finest examples of Danish design in every aspect of their stay, even when they had breakfast or dinner. Unfortunately, many of the guests struggled with the streamline cutlery, so it was soon replaced with more traditional knives, forks and spoons.

Fortunately, others saw the value of the cutlery. In 1968, the American film director Stanley Kubrick had the astronauts in his futuristic sci-fi film *2001: A Space Odyssey* use AJ cutlery. That made it world-famous.

The cutlery is known all over the world because it is so different from ordinary cutlery, not because it is particularly nice to eat with. Fortunately, it is great for many other purposes. The knife makes an excellent screw driver, and the narrow spoon is great for getting the last little bit of Nutella out of the jar.

There is plenty of cutlery in the world, so maybe Jacobsen was so forward-looking that he designed the AJ cutlery for the food people will eat in the future, which has not even been invented yet.

Monkey see, monkey do

Copy or inspiration?

Have you ever made a drawing only to see someone else copy your idea? Sometimes it feels nice, because it means they liked your drawing. But it can also be annoying if you just had a unique and special idea and you feel that the other person has nicked it.

It is difficult to say where ideas come from or who 'owns' a particular idea. But certainly, we are always inspired by someone else, even when we think we're coming up with something brand new.

It is no different for designers. As you can read in this book, Kaare Klint was inspired by Chinese paper lamps when he designed the Fruit lamp, Børge Mogensen was inspired by both chaise longues and day beds when he designed the Spoke-Back sofa and Hans J. Wegner was inspired by at least four different chair types when he designed the Wishbone chair. They all took the best elements of things they liked when they wanted to design something new.

When we use other people's experiences as a basis for our own work in this way, we call it inspiration or 'standing on the shoulders of others'. We look to others' experience because there is no point in reinventing the wheel.

However, some designers see others copying their designs directly. It is illegal to copy someone else's design, because it means that the original designers do not get paid for their work, and often the cheap copies can make the original product less valuable. Not everyone understands why they should pay much more for the original product if they can have a copy that looks almost the same for a lot less.

Copying could be called stealing ideas. In order to protect their work from being copied, designers can take out a patent. A patent can be given to new and unique elements – for example, the material the first milk cartons were made of or the construction of the Kevi castor. Someone who holds a patent owns the idea, and if anyone copies it, the original designer can prove that he or she has the legal rights to it.

There are constantly new court cases about the copying of design products. Fritz Hansen, the furniture company that makes the Egg chair and the Ant chair, among other furniture designs, sues many companies every year for copying their products.

However, a court case is always a long, hard struggle, and sometimes it can be difficult to prove that you were the first to have a particular idea.

Danish design has always had a close dialogue with the rest of the world. Designers have gone into the world and been inspired by patterns, colours, materials and crafts techniques and have taken the new influences home with them, creating their own personal expression.

Designers from other countries also come to Denmark to find inspiration here.

Nature, books, film, art, cities, food and music have inspired the development of new designs. Many impressions can be gathered using a mobile phone in the form of photos, notes and short video clips. Many designers gather inspiration in a sketchbook they carry with them. Maybe you would like to record your ideas in a sketchbook. Here you can make a collection of drawings, magazine and newspaper clippings and ideas that you can use later.

It is good to be inspired by others and to use and share each other's ideas, because that helps us to develop new knowledge. At the same time, it is also important to find your own style and to trust in your own work and ideas. It's better to be a good original than a bad copy.

A simple egg

If we had to
pick one chair as the
ultimate superstar, it would
have to be Arne Jacobsen's Egg chair.
The easy chair with the soft curves and
feminine lines has starred in more photographs
than most other furniture pieces in the world. That is
not surprising because the chair is shaped like a sculpture
and has a fascinating look from every angle.

The Egg is a large oval shell upholstered with leather or fabric and
balanced on a delicate steel base. It was designed for the SAS Royal
Hotel, which was also designed by Jacobsen. The hotel was Denmark's
first-ever skyscraper and is just across from Copenhagen's Central Station.

If you have ever sat inside a small cave or a pillow fort, perhaps you can image
what it is like to sit in the Egg. The chair embraces you and almost forms its own
private little space in a room, where you can sit undisturbed, sheltered from the
outside world. You are in a world of your own when you sit in the chair. That
makes the Egg a brilliant chair for a hotel lobby, where people might want a little
privacy while they can see what is going on around them.

Fancy hotels are not the only place where you might find the Egg. In 2007, the
burger chain McDonald's equipped some of their restaurants with the chair.
Some people thought the idea of mixing good design with fast food was
shocking. Others thought it was cool to be able to enjoy a burger in one of
the most famous chairs in the world. When it turned out the burger chain
had mixed genuine Egg chairs with copies, many people called them
out on it, and the restaurant got rid of the chairs.

Although it is a large chair, the Egg shape seems light.
In Jacobsen's own words, the form is so
simple he could have peed it in the
snow.

LEGO: play well

Probably you and your friends have all played with LEGO bricks. I hope so, because it may be the best toy ever made, and for 60 years the beloved toy brick has been a favourite of children and curious grown-ups all over the world, because it speaks to our creativity through both play and learning. The brilliant quality of the LEGO bricks is that they can be put together again and again to construct new objects. Truly, your imagination is the only limitation.

LEGO was created by Ole Kirk Christiansen, a carpenter from Jutland. At first, he made wooden toys, which soon became very popular, but he wanted to expand his company with something new. At the time, plastic had just been invented, and plastic toys were rare. Christiansen invested in a machine that could cast things in plastic, and soon the company began to make LEGO bricks. Many were sceptical of the modern material, but it soon turned out that the little bricks were a fun and challenging toy.

Since the LEGO brick was invented, LEGO has made so many toy bricks that if they were shared evenly among everyone living in Denmark, we would each have more than 100,000 LEGO bricks – enough bricks for each of us to build a tower that is one kilometre tall! LEGO has developed from a small company that made little plastic bricks to the world's biggest toy producer, which now sells everything from robots to computer games, all of it based on LEGO.

The name LEGO comes from a contraction of the first two letters in the Danish words 'leg godt', play well. Later, Christiansen realized that this also means 'I put together' in Latin. A perfect name for the LEGO bricks.

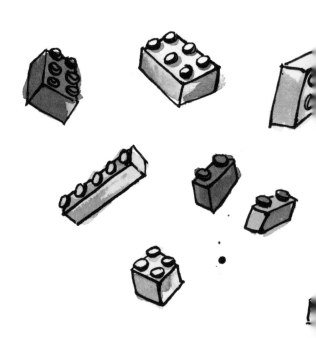

Panton chair · Verner Panton, 1958–67

A cheeky tongue

Many designers have dreamed of making a chair in a single piece of material, because it is a difficult technical challenge. In 1960, after experimenting for years, the Danish designer Verner Panton was the first person in the world to make a chair in a single piece, a single material, a single form and a single cast. What made the chair possible was plastic, a brand-new material at the time. However, the chair was not put into production until 1967, after years of challenging development work, and it took another four years to find the perfect type of plastic for the chair.

In many ways, Panton followed his very own path in Danish furniture design. Not because he wanted to be different from everyone else, but because he was interested in and inspired by other things than most designers at the time. While others preferred natural materials and traditional craftsmanship to make their furniture, Panton loved synthetic materials, which are made in a factory. And while most others preferred muted natural colours and furnishing fabrics without patterns, Panton used the whole palette, going for maximum impact in trendy colours like red, purple and orange. He did not look to earlier furnishing types, as

many of his fellow designers did, but was instead inspired by contemporary cartoons and pop culture. His style was provocative with its experimental, playful expression, and it was quite different from the serious furniture style that was dominant at the time.

Panton worked with Arne Jacobsen when Jacobsen designed the Ant chair, which you know from this book. If you look carefully at the drawing, you can see that the Panton chair has an organic form that is somewhat similar to the Ant. But perhaps most of all it resembles a giant tongue.

Panton was more interested in form than in function, and whether the Panton chair is actually comfortable is open to debate. The smooth plastic is cold and hard, and you risk getting a damp bum, because plastic cannot absorb the warm moisture from the body. Nevertheless, the English supermodel Kate Moss appeared stark naked on a Panton chair on the cover of the fashion magazine *Vogue* in 1995.

Panton wanted to make a child-sized version of the chair, but sadly he died before it was realized. The child-sized chair was put into production in 2006, eight years after Panton's death.

54

Switch and socket ·
Lauritz Knudsen (model LK 61), 1961

Switched on

A light switch is a design you touch several times a day, without even thinking about it. As a special design feature, a light switch should be discrete yet easy to find. It should look nice without being noticed. And it should clearly signal what is the right way to use it.

When it comes to light switches and electrical sockets, three things in particular have to come together: safety, function and quality. Above all, electrical sockets and switches have to be safe to use so we do not risk getting shocked when we use them. Next, they should be easy to operate. And finally, they should last for years, because they are tricky to replace.

An electric switch-and-socket set includes the button you push and an outlet with two or three holes that you can insert a plug into – for example, to charge your mobile phone.

The LK 61 switch-and-socket set is made of a type of plastic that does not melt at high temperatures. That is a good feature when we are dealing with electricity. Over the years, the Lauritz Knudsen company has developed many different switches and sockets in a wide variety of colours, materials and shapes. The original switch-and-socket set called LK 61 is now only found in older buildings.

This switch-and-socket set from Lauritz Knudsen is a classic example of Danish design. The clean, simple expression could never shock anyone.

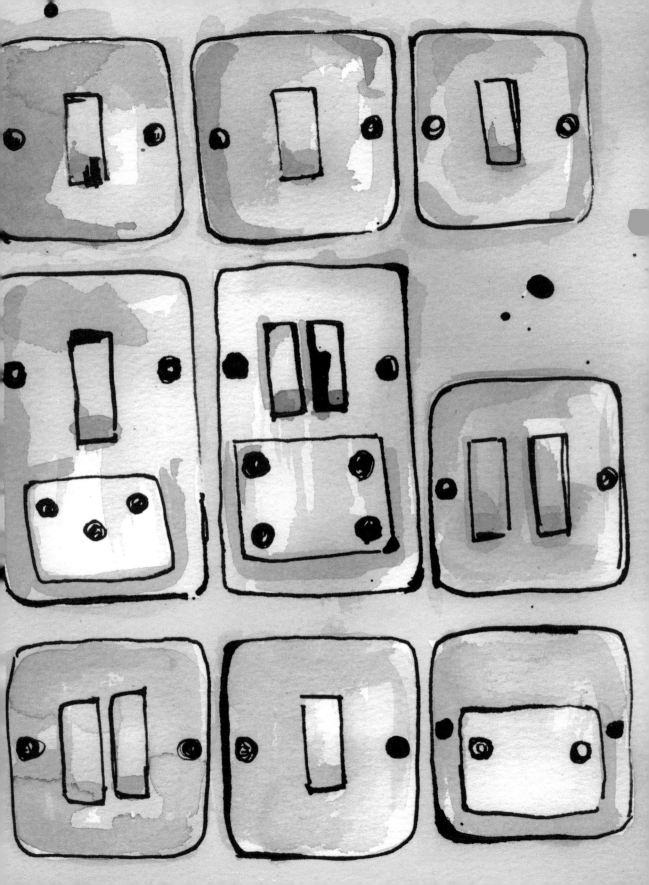

The best seat in the house

Many designs are such a natural part of everyday life that we never give them a second thought. But imagine a world without toilet seats – what would we do? The mere thought of resting one's thighs on the cold porcelain rim is enough to give most people goosebumps. In 1954, two friends, Holger Christensen and Christian Larsen, founded a company together to produce wooden toilet seats. This was before toilet seats made of plastic and other materials had been invented. They called the company Pressalit.

The first toilet seats they made were in wood – but then something unexpected happened. One evening, a cat was padding through the carpentry workshop. While playing with wood shavings and wood chips, it accidentally knocked over a jar of glue.

The glue flowed down over a hot radiator and ended up in a pile of sawdust. When the mix of glue and sawdust set, the result was a new and very strong material, which proved perfect for ... toilet seats. A chemical engineer spent two years developing and refining the material, which was named urea-plastic, and then it was ready for use. What at first seemed like an accident actually led to a major toilet seat adventure and a pioneering design.

Pressalit's goal was to turn the toilet seat into a design object of high aesthetic quality. Denmark's first proper designer toilet seat was created by Sigvard Bernadotte and Acton Bjørn and was launched on the market in 1966. In their design, they considered how we actually sit on a toilet seat to make it as comfortable as possible – something that had not been a major concern before. Since then, Pressalit has worked with some of Denmark's best designers. That has resulted in some interesting designs, including a special toilet seat for the American superstar Madonna. It looks like a flattened disco ball and adds glamour to a toilet visit.

Many people think toilet visits are a deeply private topic, even though we all have to go several times a day. Because we use the toilet so often, it is a good thing for all of us that skilled designers have spent time and effort on developing good, functional toilet seats.

Kubus candlestick · Mogens Lassen, 1962

A cube of air

When designers create a product, they also have to come up with a name for it. Many designers use their initials and a number, like the PH 5 lamp and the PK22 chair that we encountered earlier in this book. Others prefer to have a name that describes the new object. Kubus means 'cube' in Latin and is a good name for this candlestick, which is shaped exactly like a cube.

Functionalism is a principle in design and architecture that is focused on simple forms and materials. The style became popular in Denmark during the 1940s and has played an important role in Danish design ever since. When you look at the Kubus candlestick, which was designed by Mogens Lassen in 1962, maybe you can see that he was a functionalist and an architect. The straight lines and regular form of the cube make the candlestick look like a simplified house without walls, a box constructed of sharp metal rods that are painted black. On this metal frame rounded candleholders have been mounted.

Originally, Lassen designed the Kubus candlestick as a gift he could give to his family and friends. It was only when his grandson Søren Lassen put it into production in 1994 that it became available in the shops – for all of us.

The candlestick has a very simple form, like a naked frame where everything superfluous has been removed. When Lassen created it, the candlestick was very different from other candlesticks, which often had rounded shapes to signal *hygge* – a warm, cosy mood. Kubus has a pared-down form that seems the opposite of *hygge*. But it is a good match for many modern homes, and it combines a square, regular construction with warm, homely candlelight.

Toadstool · Nanna Ditzel, 1962

Where did the toad go?

Do you know the feeling when you just cannot sit still on a chair? That is quite normal, and in fact most children cannot sit still for very long. Children move, slide around, curl up and lounge in ways that many grown-ups forget is just natural for a child. That was why Nanna Ditzel designed the Toadstool in 1962. In her own home, she had seen her three children play on the furniture and noticed how they never sat still for five minutes. That was her inspiration.

The Toadstool is toy and furniture in one, it can be used as a chair or as a table and you can roll it and stack it. The shape invites you to move freely because it does not have legs or a backrest like traditional furniture. It is light enough that a child can move it without help, and it is milled in solid wood without any visible joints where you might pinch your fingers.

Ditzel was one of the first women to play a major role in Danish design. She was tired of boxy furniture with straight lines. She thought furniture should have rounded shapes, just like human beings. Based on human shapes and forms, her furniture often added a lively and playful contrast to the right angles and straight walls of the room.

During the 1960s, Danes began to focus more on how they wanted to spend their free time, and many talked about human beings as 'homo ludens': 'playing man'. This was exactly what Ditzel wanted to do with her Toadstool: to encourage children and grown-ups to play. That is easy to see, because even though the Toadstool was originally designed for children, it also proved very popular with grown-ups.

63

Wristwatch · Ole Mathiesen, 1962

Timeless

Years, months, weeks, days, hours, minutes, seconds – we measure time all the time, and clocks and watches are important instruments for most people.

Today, many people use their mobile phone to see what time it is, but before mobile phones, it was common for both children and grown-ups to wear a wristwatch to keep track of time.

Ole Mathiesen was a trained watchmaker and had learned a lot about clockworks from his father, who was also a watchmaker, and from his apprenticeship in a Swiss watch factory. Switzerland is world-famous for making excellent but also very expensive watches. At some point, Mathiesen felt the time was right to design a quality watch that was also affordable: a good watch that was not only for the rich. He designed a simple watch with a thin white face, black hands and a leather strap.

The watch only has two hands: a minute hand and an hour hand. Mathiesen felt that a second hand would make the design too busy. He wanted to design a watch that signalled calm, order and control. The watch is an example of Scandinavian minimalism, which means it does not include any superfluous decorative features.

The simple wristwatch was created during the heyday of Danish design and has remained in production ever since. With a paradoxical term, you could say that the watch is 'timeless', even though it is of course designed to tell time.

Bow chair · Grete Jalk, 1963

Feminine folds

It is hard to imagine how a chair could have anything to do with equality between men and women, but the Bow chair did. The chair was designed by Grete Jalk in 1963. At a time when almost all the trained furniture designers or cabinetmakers were men, Grete Jalk was something unusual as a female cabinetmaker.

She designed the Bow chair for a British furniture competition. The task was to design a chair for a man and one for a woman. Jalk designed two shell chairs in moulded laminated wood and won first prize. The feminine chair, which has soft lines that reminds us of a woman's body, was especially well received, and the Museum of Modern Art in New York immediately bought one, which they still have on display today.

If you look carefully at the drawing, you can see that the Bow chair looks almost like a human body, with a back, a waist and hips. The chair for a man

was never quite as popular, and it was never put into production.

The Bow chair has a very unusual construction. It is made of only two pieces of laminated wood: one that forms the seat and one that forms the back. At the bottom, the two pieces are discreetly joined together with a tiny metal screw. The form is so simple and natural that it looks like a soft and loosely tied silk bow.

Because of the unusual look, only 300 Bow chairs were ever made. Today it is considered an important element in Danish chair design history, and it has been put into production again. An original chair costs more than 30,000 euros today because they are so rare.

In the past, it was difficult for women to get an education or a career as a designer. Jalk was a pioneer who helped change that. Today, there are about equal numbers of women and men who are designers in Denmark.

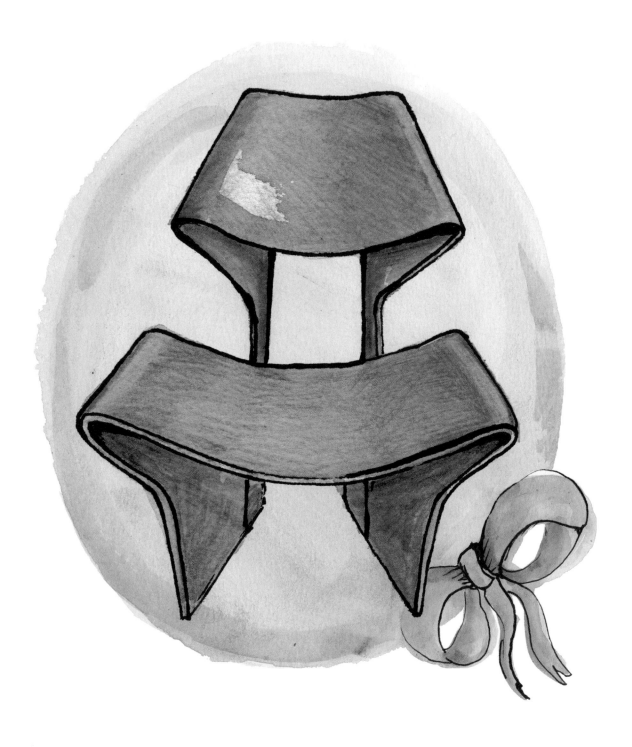

A democratic table

What do the Olympic Stadium in Mexico City, a large city square in Stockholm and a popular Danish dining table have in common? If you look carefully at the drawing, you will find the answer.

All three are so-called superellipses: a geometric shape that was developed by Danish designer, poet and visionary Piet Hein.

Hein invented the superellipse for the city square Sergels Torg in Stockholm, Sweden. The city council wanted a shape that was neither round nor square. After considering what geometric shape might work, Piet Hein came up with the mathematical formula for a shape that is in between an oval and a rectangle. He called it the superellipse.

The Olympic Stadium in Mexico City, high-rise developments in Chicago and the swimming hall in DGI-byen in Copenhagen are all large-scale versions of Hein's superellipse, but the Super-Elliptical table is probably what he is best known for. The tabletop in the characteristic superellipse shape is made of chipboard covered with a hard laminate and an aluminium edge. The legs are made of thin stainless-steel rods.

Because there is no clearly marked head of the Super-Elliptical table, there does not have to be any discussion about who should sit at the head of the table. That is why Hein proposed it as a meeting table for the peace talks in Paris in 1968 between the United States and North and South Vietnam during the Vietnam War. Even before the talks began, the parties had been unable to agree on who was going to sit at the head of the table.

A large Super-Elliptical table with room for 24 persons was ordered, but due to problems with delivery, Hein's table was rejected in favour of another. However, the story lives on and has helped promote the story about the Super-Elliptical table as a democratic table where all seats are equal.

In the weave

Fabric, cloth and textile all mean the same thing. Designers often use the word 'fabric'.

Have you ever thought about the fact that all the fabrics we use for clothes, tea towels, bed linen and furniture upholstery are designed by someone? Materials, patterns and colours were all developed by a designer who put his or her time and imagination into creating them.

Nanna Ditzel was mainly a furniture designer, but she also designed fabrics. Her most famous fabric is Hallingdal. The fabric feels a little scratchy if you sit on it wearing shorts or a short skirt because it is woven of 70% wool and 30% viscose. That makes for a durable material and lets the colours come through nice and bright. Furniture fabrics have to be hardwearing so they do not tear, and the colours have to stay bright so the furniture does not look dull and faded. Wool and viscose are two of the best materials on these two counts. If the fabric is a little scratchy, that is the price you have to pay.

The Hallingdal fabric is made on a large loom, where the individual threads are woven into fabric. The weave used for the Hallingdal fabric is called a linen weave. It is a good choice when you need a textile that lasts for years because it makes for a sturdy, hardwearing fabric. Linen weave is the simplest weave that exists; it consists in simply weaving one thread over another. To see an example of a linen weave, you can look at a linen or cotton bed sheet through a magnifying glass.

Although most designers dream of making a good product that many people enjoy using, Ditzel probably had not imagined that almost every-one in Denmark would come into contact with her Hallingdal fabric at some point or another. Since the fabric was designed in 1965, it has been used for everything from chairs and sofas in private homes to seat upholstery in cars, theatres and concert halls. If you have ever travelled on a Danish IC3 train, you have sat on a seat uphol-stered with Hallingdal.

Ditzel loved colours – especially pink, red and orange, and Hallingdal was designed in more than 100 different colourways. Although there are so many colours to choose from, the greys and blacks are in fact the most popular.

Kevi castor · Jørgen Rasmussen, 1965

On a roll

Have you felt the rush of shooting across the floor on a high-speed office chair? From the moment you push off with your feet until you arrive at your goal, it's a fast, smooth ride. The reason why it rolls that well is the Kevi castor.

A castor is the small set of wheels attached to some furniture – for example, office chairs. Before Kevi, castors were unstable and noisy and did not run very smooth. They also scratched the floor and had to be lubricated with oil because they were made of metal. In short, they were far from great. The idea for the Kevi castor arose in connection with the design of the famous Kevi chair. Designer Jørgen Rasmussen saw a chance to improve the castors for office chairs and began to draw sketches and develop prototypes. It took a lot of work and good drawing skills, imagination and knowledge about form and function.

The result was a double castor that is able to swivel on its own axis and move freely in any direction. This makes office chairs easier to move, more flexible and much more practical. The castor also does not scratch the floor, and it is almost silent.

The Kevi castor has improved life for millions of children and adults who spend many hours each day sitting on an office chair. It is a good example that good design can sometimes seem so obvious that we do not even notice it. Since 1965, the Kevi castor has been developed further, and now there are special models adapted to both rugs and wooden floors.

More than a billion Kevi castors have been sold, and it is the most common – and the most copied – office chair castor in the world.

Nørgaard T-shirt (model 101) · Jørgen Nørgaard, 1967

Rebel rib

Imagine what it would be like to feel cold all the time when you were indoors. Many Danish homes used to be cold because flats and houses did not have proper insulation. In winter, many people wore big sweaters indoors to stay warm.

That changed during the 1960s when most homes were insulated and had radiators put in. Houses got warmer, and people needed clothes that were less warm. That gave Jørgen Nørgaard, who in 1958 had opened the fashion shop Nørgaard paa Strøget, the idea to design a long-sleeved T-shirt for women in soft, elastic cotton rib.

Nørgaard was inspired by Hollywood film stars who had worn T-shirts in some of the major films of the time. He thought that looked cool. It was also a little provocative at the time because T-shirts were not normal streetwear – and certainly not for women. Women rarely wore clothes that clung to the body because they were not supposed to show off their figure. That may seem hard to imagine today.

The youth revolt and the women's liberation movement made the T-shirt much more popular. Many young people rejected existing norms and traditions, including ideas about how women should dress. In that way, the T-shirt took on political meaning, because women had never worn tight-fitting clothes before. It offered a liberated and relaxed style with its body-hugging simplicity and became the symbol of a new feminism.

In a very original move, the T-shirt was named after the major American highway Route 101. Many associated the American highways with exuberance and freedom, qualities that Nørgaard wanted the T-shirt to represent, in both a symbolic and a practical sense. Because the body of the T-shirt is knit in a single piece there are no irritating or scratchy side seams, so you can move with complete freedom. The sleeves are sewn on afterwards.

Although the original model 101 was only made in one size, women of all shapes and sizes have loved it ever since it was launched in 1967, and more than three million T-shirts have been sold. The only things that have changed over the years are the colours and the addition of a child-size model. By now, the 101 T-shirt has become a Danish design icon, just like the Ant chair and the Margrethe bowl, and it will probably never go out of fashion.

The daily news

Do you ever read a newspaper? If you do, you probably read it online, where it is quick and easy to get your daily news. There are many activities competing for the readers' time, and to be successful, media have to stand out from their competition. A newspaper has to have a strong graphic profile – whether in print or in the digital world. A graphic profile is also called a layout and has to do with the design of letters, pictures, colours and sections of text. The goal is to make the content accessible and interesting.

Politiken was originally a print news-paper, and it has been around for donkey's years – a really long time. Since 1884, in fact. At first it was almost all text, but with technical development more and more pictures, colours and drawings showed up on the pages. After a while, the layout had become so messy that it had to be cleaned up. In 1968, the graphic designer Austin Grandjean renewed *Politiken*'s style and simplified the general impression. He chose a typeface that was easy to read. The pages had more white space and were less cluttered, which improved the reading experience. In many ways, the layout followed the same principle as classic Danish furniture: 'less is more'.

Politiken has repeatedly won the award as the world's best designed newspaper because it has an aesthe-tically appealing presentation of text, drawings, layout and photographs. Some even think that the graphic profile is the reason it continues to attract and appeal to readers.

Politiken's graphic design is used both in print and online, and it works both in the large format of the newspaper page and in the small format of a smartphone screen. It is important to have a uniform expression across all the different platforms to make the product recognizable to the reader.

Today, we can use our computers and smartphones to get news from across the globe just a few seconds after something has happened. Therefore, most people do not read print newspapers in order to get breaking news but to get the background story and because they enjoy sitting down with a paper. And even though print newspapers have long been under threat from digital media, it does seem that print newspapers are here to stay – even though the fresh ink can turn your fingers black.

Luminous flowers

The Flowerpot lamp was created when the hippie culture and flower children were in full bloom. Young people were rejecting old norms and traditions and expressing a new way of life through colourful clothes and non-violent protests under the slogan 'Make love not war'. This was the time when the first people landed on the Moon, and The Beatles was one of the most popular bands among young people. These events may explain why the lamp is called Flowerpot: a safe place for flowers to thrive and bloom and spread colour and joy to their surroundings. That was characteristic of the style of the designer who created the lamp, Verner Panton. To Panton, freedom and exuberance, expressed through colours, were fundamental values. The name also refers to the flower power movement, which was into hallucinogenic drugs, psychedelic music and free love.

Panton was a furniture designer, and as we saw earlier, he was one of the first Danish designers to combine bright colours, plastic and geometric shapes. When he designed the Flowerpot lamp, he experimented with hollow metal balls. One day, he cut the balls in half and experimented with combining them in new ways.

Two hemispheres in thin enamelled metal, one twice as big as the other, became the Flowerpot design. The hemispheres face each other, creating a lampshade that hides the light bulb from view and prevents glare. A clever detail is that the top hemispheres is painted white inside, while the inside of the bottom one is orange. When the lamp is switched on, this gives the light a soft, warm reddish tone.

Panton followed his own way instead of following the style or the way of designing that was common at the time in Denmark. This made it difficult for him to be accepted, so he left Denmark and made his career abroad. His work includes big interior designs in high-intensity colours. It was only after his death that design enjoyed a revival in Denmark, and several of his designs have now been put back into production.

Panton was a colourful personality who argued that there should be a special tax on white paint to make it more expensive than other colours because white is so boring. Knowing that, it may sound strange that he chose to design his Flowerpot in red, orange, turquoise, blue – and white.

d line · Knud Holscher, 1971

Interior accessories

Have you ever looked carefully at the door handles in your home? Are they all the same? What are they made of, what colour are they, and do they fit well into your hand? Door handles are an example of the fairly anonymous designs we use every day. They belong to a product category known as architectural hardware or architectural ironmongery (even if they are made of plastic). Maybe you do not know what that means. Architectural hardware includes many of the things that need to work in a building without drawing too much attention to themselves, including door handles, coat hooks, keyhole covers, toilet roll holders and door stops. Together, these things are all called industrial design. They are important design objects that make it easy and hassle-free to carry out everyday functions such as opening a door, tearing off some sheets of toilet paper and hanging your jacket on a hook.

Designer and architect Knud Holscher saw a need and decided to design a whole series of architectural hardware in stainless steel. For the project, he used a new technique that made it possible to bend steel pipes in a sharp angle. That allowed for brand-new clean, angular shapes that he thought would work well in a building. Because all the parts were designed as part of a series and had the same expression, they looked good together. The different items had to be easy to install and use, and they should not draw attention away from the building itself.

One of the features that make d line unique is quite technical, so fasten your seat belt: the diameter of the pipe is the same as the diameter of the interior circle of the bend. The consistent design and the simple material give the series a uniform expression, which is a good feature, because d line has grown to include more than 2,000 different parts, all of which go well together. In fact, it is the world's biggest design series. It is used in many private homes, in Copenhagen Airport, at the British Museum in London and many other places around the world.

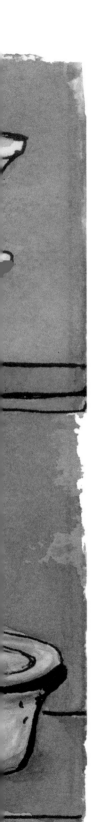

Firepot · Grethe Meyer, 1976

Fire and ice

Most families have days when they have to get dinner ready in a hurry with a minimum of mess or have dirty dishes to be cleaned afterwards. That is nothing new – that happened 50 years ago too.

Developments in society create new needs and inspire designers to come up with new and better products. In the 1970s, more women entered the labour market. Previously, many women had stayed at home looking after the children, but now they were getting jobs outside the home and began to earn their own money. The children were put into day care, and that changed everyday life in the family.

Now that everybody was away at work during the day, there was less time to cook. That called for new solutions, since pre-packaged dinners and takeaways were far less common than today.

To save time, people needed bowls and dishes that could go straight from the freezer to the oven and which looked nice enough to be used for serving. To meet that need, designer Grete Meyer created the stoneware series Firepot with more than 30 different items, including bowls, dishes and ramekins. The series was made of a clay mixture called cordierite, which can handle great variations in temperature. However, the material cannot be glazed, and it changes colour with use over time. Some would call that wear and tear, meaning that it is damaged or deteriorates; others would call it patina, meaning that it gets more beautiful with age.

Firepot became an instant success, but, soon after, disposable trays made of aluminium foil became popular, and the interest in Firepot fell. Today, Firepot is no longer in production, but it is popular among people who collect Danish design. If you see a brown, unglazed bowl or dish in a charity shop, you may have discovered an original Firepot.

A coffee-table bird

A small beak, a round black eye and a wing. Seen in profile, the Stelton vacuum jug looks like a stylized bird.

The jug was originally designed for Stelton's popular series Cylinda Line, which was designed by Arne Jacobsen. He passed away before he could design a vacuum jug for the series, so the task passed instead to the designer Erik Magnussen. Magnussen wanted to create an elegant jug that would keep the contents hot and which looked so nice that people would want to put it on the table. At the time, many people used tall, slender porcelain jugs to serve coffee. Vacuum jugs were not used in the home, only for picnics. Magnussen wanted to change that.

If you look at the shape, you can see that he really took the name, Cylinda Line, literally. As you can see in the drawing, the jug is a simple cylinder that is only interrupted by a small spout and a handle. In design language, you would say that it is an example of the modernist preference of geometric shapes.

Vacuum jugs consist of an exterior, the part we can see, and an interior, the part inside that keeps the liquid hot. To make sure the Stelton jug was not too costly to make, Magnussen used a standard vacuum flask for the interior. These flasks were tall and narrow, so the shape of the Stelton jug was tall and narrow too. For the jug, he invented a special lid that tilts open when you tip the jug to pour and seals tight when the jug is set upright on the table again. This lets you use the jug with just one hand. The jug is designed to be used indoors, at a table. It is not practical on a picnic because the lid is not held in place, so if the jug tips over, the hot coffee pours out. Therefore, a doctor demanded that the jug be recalled from the shops because he saw a risk that children might get scalded; in 1989, Stelton launched a new model with a lid that screws down.

The tilt lid was a technical innovation, but in aesthetic terms Magnussen also broke with tradition. All decoration had been removed, and all that remained was a simple jug with an unusually tall and slender body. The entire world has embraced the Stelton jug, probably because the simple design is timeless, in many ways, as well as very distinctive, but probably also because the jug is continually launched in new colours, so that it keeps up with changing fashions.

Hot food, cool design

Good food makes people happy, and if it is prepared with love and beautifully arranged, it seems to taste even better. During the 1970s, many Danes had begun to take more trips abroad where they found inspiration for new dishes they could serve at home. The new food called for new pots and pans that were better than the ones that were already on the market.

Ole Palsby, who had previously had a kitchenware shop, was asked to design a series of pots for this new market. With inspiration from the regular, geometric forms of the Bauhaus School, he designed a series of simple, cylindrical pots and pans.

Palsby based this series, which was called Eva Trio, on his knowledge that no single material is perfect for all kinds of cooking. Different materials differ in the way they conduct heat, so he decided to use the different properties of three different metals to design the best pots and pans.

He used aluminium, copper and cast iron. Aluminium is good for pots that are used to boil things – for example, potatoes. Copper is great for small saucepans that are used for quickly heating up a sauce. Cast iron can get very hot and is ideal for frying pans because it can give meat a nice, crisp crust.

All the handles are made of stainless steel and are shaped as long grips riveted on to the pots and lids. Because the contact surface between the pot or pan and the grip is so small, the grip does not get hot. This means that it is safe to touch, even without using a potholder. The grip can also be used to hang the pots, pans and lids on a hook.

Today, most people in Denmark are familiar with Eva Trio, but when the series was launched, it was an innovation. The design is still popular today, and many families still use the original pots that were made during the 1970s. So when we say that a design is 'durable', it means both that the design stays modern and that the product holds up to daily use.

Maybe you are wondering who Eva Trio was? She never existed. The manufacturer of the series was the company Eva Denmark, and because the series uses three metals, it was named Eva Trio.

AIR Titanium glasses frame ·
Teit Weylandt and Hans Dissing, 1986

I can see clearly now

Maybe you know what it is like not to be able to see quite clearly. If you do not, you can try to squint a little until things begin to look blurry. Poor eyesight can feel a little like that. Luckily, we can fix that by getting the right glasses.

In the past, children did not get glasses. They were expensive, and children were thought to have good eyesight because their eyes were young and had not seen much use. People did not need glasses until they were old and their eyes were worn out.

So originally, glasses for children were really designed for grown-ups. They were big, with a clunky metal frame and thick lenses made of real glass. They were a drag to wear because they were heavy and fitted poorly, so they slid around. They were cumbersome to wear while playing, and you always had to be careful because the glass might shatter if the glasses fell on the ground.

During the past 50 years, designers have created glasses specially for children – ones that match children's size and needs. They are light, flexible, sturdy and stylish.

The AIR Titanium frame was originally designed for grown-ups by Teit Weyland and Hans Dissing in cooperation with Lindberg Optik in 1986. The unique thing about the AIR Titanium frame is that it is made of titanium, a super-lightweight material that is also used in the aerospace industry. A titanium frame weighs only three grams, which makes it one of the lightest glasses frames in the world.

Dissing was so pleased with the new frame that he thought it would be good for children too. In 1993, together with Otto Weitling and Lindberg Optik, he designed RIM, a series of titanium frames for children. Although titanium is a metal, it is slightly elastic. That makes it a brilliant material for children's glasses frames, because it can be adjusted until it fits perfectly. This means you do not have to think about the fact that you are wearing glasses and you can simply be yourself. And because the frame is almost invisible, you do not notice the glasses but see the person instead.

A colourful family

Many good designs are inspired by everyday life and things that are close to us. That is also the case with Ursula, a table service that was designed by the ceramicist Ursula Munch-Petersen in 1991. Ever since her childhood on the Danish island of Bornholm in the Baltic Sea, she has been interested in plants and animals. The oval plates, yellow cups with green handles and a jug with a spout that looks like a bird's beak reflect her love of nature's organic forms, colours and vitality.

Maybe Munch-Pedersen had a bird in mind when she designed the jug. With its chubby body and cheeky beak, it looks like a duck, and it has a touch of humour that can light up a grey day. The whole service is based on the same asymmetric and funky shapes that give it a family likeness, even though the parts have different colours.

The designer describes the set as simple and ordinary, and she calls it 'the everyday service'. She wants to show us that ordinary is not the same as boring. With the service, she wants to remind us to use our senses, live a simple life and appreciate our everyday life and surroundings. That is best done by living a calm and focused life. Maybe you think it sounds like reading a lot of meaning into a table service, but designers often put many thoughts into their work. Every design represents years of work, thoughts and intentions. Often that goes well beyond what we can see, but maybe we can sense it. And that is probably why some things become more important to us than others: because we sense that the designer put a lot of thought and effort into making them.

Because Munch-Petersen put so many thoughts and so much work into the design, her intentions shine through the colourful glazes. That is probably why the service carries her own name, Ursula.

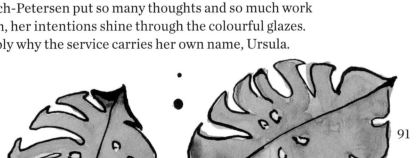

Washing up in style

For most people, washing the dishes is just a tedious chore. That was also how the ceramicist Ole Jensen felt about it. He decided to find a way to make it more pleasant, perhaps even fun, to clean the dishes. Today, many people have a dishwasher, but before then everyone cleaned their dishes by hand. If you have ever tried to clean a large oven dish, you will know

what a hassle it can be to try to cram it into the washing-up bowl. That was one of Jensen's challenges. He also did not like the hard, clanging noise that metal and porcelain can make in a washing-up bowl of hard plastic. He wanted to make a bowl that adapted to the dishes that had to be cleaned, rather than the other way round. So he decided

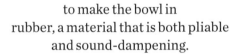

to make the bowl in rubber, a material that is both pliable and sound-dampening.

Through many experiments, he found that the soft sides of a rubber bowl were just too flexible. So he stabilized the bowl by folding down the top edge, as some people do when they fold down the top edge of a pair of wellingtons. The bend produced the characteristic edge.

Traditionally, washing-up bowls have anonymous plastic products that few people paid much attention to. Something that was kept out of sight under the kitchen sink. Jensen changed that. He turned it into a design object and created perhaps the world's most expensive washing-up bowl. It costs about 25 times as much as a plastic washing-up bowl. But the price has not scared off the customers. On the contrary.

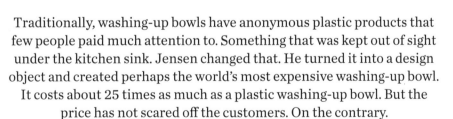

The bowl has become popular around the world and has even been used as a wine cooler at the Museum of Modern Art in New York. Others have discovered that it's great for footbaths, as a box for keeping toys in or as a place to store food items in the kitchen. Maybe you can come up with even more things it could be used for?

Mega modern pattern

Danish design is not known for its use of patterns, but there is one exception: blue fluted porcelain. The blue floral pattern, which most Danes will recognize, is still painted by hand, as it has been since 1775. Each blue fluted plate takes 762 brushstrokes done with the finest brushes made of the hairs from the very tip of a cow's ear.

Then, 225 years after it was created, blue fluted had a baby sister: Blue Fluted Mega, designed by ceramicist Karen Kjældgård-Larsen. When she created it, she was still a student, about to do her graduation project at The Danish Design School.

As a child she loved the blue fluted pattern. She drew it on writing paper and dreamed of becoming a blue fluted painter when she grew up. So for her graduation project, she chose to work with the pattern. But how to improve on something you love?

Kjældgård-Larsen took the blue fluted pattern and blew it up as if it were seen through a magnifying glass. Then she painted elements of the pattern on white plates and called it Blue Fluted Mega. With this new design, she breathed new life into the traditional porcelain pattern while preserving its aesthetic qualities.

After graduating, she presented her idea to Royal Copenhagen – the company that produces the Blue Fluted porcelain. The company loved her innovation and made a contract to produce six different Blue Fluted Mega plates. They were a huge success.

Since then, the oversize blue fluted pattern has been painted on more than a hundred different products, from cups to dishes, cake stands and jugs. Kjældgård-Larsen is still the one who decides how the clear, blue flowers are to unfold on the porcelain. Today, when we see the result of her work, it seems so natural and straightforward. But when she created the Mega design, it was a brand-new idea.

This story illustrates that you do not necessarily have to be experienced in order to come up with a great design. It is just as important to focus on something you love and to believe in your ideas.

Caravaggio · Cecilie Manz, 2005

A bright red line

When Cecilie Manz sets out to design something new, she always begins with pen and paper. The sketching phase, when her ideas take shape as drawings, is the basis for her work. Later, the sketches are scanned and transferred to a computer.

When she designed the Caravaggio lamp, her design process also began at the drawing table. She wanted to design a lamp that highlighted the lamp cord instead of trying to hide it, as we normally do. She designed a bell shape that was open at both ends so that both the cord and the surroundings were lit. This means that the cord became part of the actual lamp design. When the cord is put on the spot like this, it has to look nice. That is why Caravaggio is fitted with an eye-catching red fabric cord.

You may not normally notice electrical cords and cables much, but take a look at the ones in your home. Most are probably covered with black, grey or white plastic. They are often hidden because they are not normally very pretty. In recent years, many new lamps have appeared with coloured cords, and in fact Verner Panton used coloured cords when he designed the Flowerpot lamp back in 1968.

Caravaggio is a so-called pendant lamp: a lamp that hangs down from the ceiling. It soon became a success, probably in part because the red cord gives it a characteristic and somewhat unusual look.

And the name? It refers to the Italian baroque painter Caravaggio, who is known for paintings with a high contrast between light and dark – just like Manz's lamp. Out of the darkness comes the light!

Veryround · Louise Campbell, 2006

Round and round we go

You should know the Veryround chair because it is a good example of how designers play with form, material and technique.

You might wonder whether Veryround is in fact a chair or an experiment with form. Louise Campbell, who designed it, calls it a chair, for even though it does not have legs, a seat and a back, you could actually sit in it. It embraces the body with its open form and has proportions that match the human scale. Few people have ever sat in the Veryround chair, as only 1,000 have actually been produced. Campbell personally signs every single chair, the way an artist signs a work of art.

Veryround is made up of more than 100 circles. The circles are both the construction of the chair and its decoration. When Campbell made the Veryround, she first experimented with models that she made using scissors, glue and paper. Next, the models were transferred to a computer program, laser-cut in two thin steel sheets and joined together at the side. You can clearly tell that Veryround was designed with the assistance of modern technology, and even if a skilled smith were to try it, the chair would be hopeless to produce by hand because the design is so technical.

Veryround is virtually an impossible piece of furniture, but it was put into production nevertheless. It might sound strange that anyone would produce or buy a chair you cannot really sit in. The point of the chair is not comfort but to be an aesthetic and eye-catching object, because Veryround is incredibly beautiful, especially when the light falls on it so you can see the pattern of the shadows.

Want to play?

In this book, we have looked at several examples of furniture designed for children. First, Hans J. Wegner's children's chair, Peter's chair, which looks like an ordinary chair, only child-sized. Next, Nanna Ditzel's Toadstool, which challenges our ideas about what a piece of furniture can be but still has one foot in the world of grown-up furniture. The bObles series goes one step further. It is play furniture designed for children, and it does not look like anything we know from the grown-up universe – not even close.

The idea for bObles was conceived by architect Bolette Blædel while she was on maternity leave with her first child. She thought there was a lack of fun rough-and-tumble furniture for children and decided to design some herself. Together with her sister, designer Louise Blædel, she created a series of furniture designed to promote children's motor development with features of form, function and colour that stimulate imagination and play.

The bObles series is made of a sturdy foam material that is firm, lightweight and soft. The material is shaped into geometric figures that look like different animals, including crocodiles, elephants, chicks and fish. The elements can rock and bob, they can be stacked, and they can be used as chairs or tables, for balancing games and for building forts. They are light and smooth as velvet and easy to move around, even for young children. Their surface prevents them from slipping on the floor, which makes them safe and stable. bObles also includes elements shaped as letters so that children can play and construct with the alphabet.

bObles is based on the belief that play, balancing and motor skills lead to happy, healthy children and that physical activity can improve children's learning and confidence. The colourful rough-and-tumble toys are sold in many other countries and enjoyed by children all over the world.

Nobody's perfect

It was a difficult task that led to the design of the Nobody chair. The Swedish prison service needed new chairs to be used in the cells.

The task was as follows: design a chair that cannot be used in a fight, that cannot be turned into a weapon, that you cannot hide anything in and that does not make any noise. The chair also had to be comfortable, work as both an easy chair and a dining chair, be easy to clean and easy to move around. How would you solve that task?

Boris Berlin and Poul Christiansen, who are behind the Komplot Design studio, accepted the challenge and designed the Nobody chair. The name is an apt description, as the chair has no body – the material is self-supporting, so the chair does not have a frame.

Although it may sound strange, the Nobody chair is made of recycled plastic bottles. The bottles are melted down and turned into fibres as thin as thread. The fibres are then laid out in thin layers on top of each other, which are tangled up with special needles. This process turns the layers into felt. At the factory, the felt undergoes a

special process that makes it stable. As part of this process, it is heated and then draped over a chair-shaped template. Once it cools the material is strong enough to keep its shape, support a human body and be used as a chair. The chair almost looks as if someone had draped a blanket over a chair, frozen it into shape and then removed the chair.

At first, Nobody was only made as an adult-sized chair, but today it is also sold as a children's chair. It is great for children because it has no sharp edges or corners that they can get hurt on, it is easy for a child to move, it does not fall over when you stand on it, and it can be used to hide under or as a small cave.

Komplot Design won many design awards for Nobody Chair, especially because the design is sustainable. However, the designers have not revealed how many plastic bottles it takes to make a chair – or how many fizzy drinks they had during the design process!

A fine balance

Sustainable design

Sustainability means that we all have to help each other keep the earth healthy so we can pass it on in a good state to all the children who have not been born yet.

Today, many designers choose to create sustainable designs. They think about what the product should be made of, how it is going to be made and whether it will be durable. They think about whether the materials are natural or can be recycled and whether the things are made in factories that do not pollute and which do not use child labour. They also think about how the product can be transported to the shops in a way that pollutes as little as possible. Sustainable design is about protecting the earth and everyone who lives here – before, during and after production.

Things that last a long time and do not go out of style are more sustainable. If we want to keep the things we own for a long time, we buy fewer new things and consume less. That is true of many of the products you can read about in this book. The Spoke-Back sofa and the Juno bed are things that are used for a long time and are then passed down to the next generation, because they are made with quality craftsmanship and in a durable design. Some even find that these products become even more beautiful and more valuable over time because they develop patina and have a history.

Many companies develop sustainable products using new materials. For example, LEGO has begun to make more sustainable toy bricks made of plastic that is based on sugar cane, which leads to less pollution than traditional plastic when the bricks are made.

But design is not just about physical objects, like toys, lamps and candlesticks. It is also about coming up with new clever solutions to specific challenges. That too can be sustainable design.

One example is Vigga, a company that was founded in 2015. Vigga tries to solve the problem of all the children's clothes that are thrown out all the time because children grow so fast. Vigga Svensson, who is the founder of the company, designs organic children's clothes that the customers rent instead of buying. Once the child has outgrown the clothes, the parents return it to the company, which sends them a new package of clothing in the right size. In this way, the parents can replace the clothes as the child grows and avoid waste. That is an example of the so-called circular economy. It is a very clever solution because it lets us consume things without producing waste.

Another example of how design can create new solutions in a world that we need to make more sustainable is the company Aarstiderne. Thomas Harttung and Søren Ejlersen wanted people living in the city to eat more fresh, organic vegetables. So in 1997, they opened an online shop that delivered organic greens straight to the customers' doorstep. That proved to be very popular, and over the years the company has grown. Today it also sells fruit, meal kits, pre-cooked meals and cook books, and it holds courses where children learn to grow vegetables and prepare healthy and sustainable meals.

Sustainability is about many different things. We need to change our mindset – the way we think. Instead of simply buying something and throwing it away when we get tired of it, we should think about what we use and how we use it. And we should consider whether the things we do not need any more might be useful to someone else. That way we can all help look after the environment and each other, both now and in the future.

Paper money is not made of paper

In Denmark, we began to use paper money, banknotes, for payment more than 300 years ago. Before then, we used coins made of copper, silver and gold. The value of a coin was based on its weight, so you needed deep pockets if you were going to buy something expensive. That has changed, and today most people in Denmark use a payment card or a mobile phone app. This is quick and convenient.

Although we use banknotes more and more rarely, they are an important Danish design, and the decoration on the notes reflects our shared history.

The current series of Danish banknotes was designed by Karin Birgitte Lund in 2009. On the front, the notes show five different Danish bridges. Each bridge was selected as a masterpiece of Danish engineering and architecture. The back shows prehistoric finds, which are examples of the earliest Danish crafts objects.

The front of the 200-krone banknote shows the Copenhagen bridge Knippelsbro. The back shows a belt plate made of bronze that was created during the Bronze Age. The bridge and the belt plate appear on the same note because the belt plate was found near the site of the bridge. The images build a bridge between past and present, tell our history and show that craftsmanship and design have always been important aspects of Danish culture.

Banknotes are difficult to make because they have to have design features that make it difficult for counterfeiters to copy them. That is why banknotes have a watermark, a secret image you can only see when you hold the note up to the light. There is also a hidden security thread of metal inside the note and a hologram to make the notes harder to copy. To make it possible for blind or partially sighted people to tell the notes apart, the 100- and 200-krone notes have slightly raised print you can feel with your fingers.

Did you know that banknotes are not made of paper? In fact, they are made of cotton. See if you can tell next time you hold a banknote. But do not wait too long – soon the banknotes may be gone because all our payments are going to be digital.

About A Chair · Hee Welling, 2010

Keep it simple

A simple shell and four legs. Haven't we seen that before? Sure, but still, About A Chair is interesting. Many consider it a new classic in Danish chair design because it is classic and modern at the same time.

In the design process, designer Hee Welling focused on his own ideas about what he wanted from a good chair. As a result, the chair has some of the same personality features as the designer: it is down-to-earth, reliable and not too precious. A simple, robust and fairly affordable chair. Ordinary, but not boring.

Actually, About A Chair is not just a chair. It is an entire family of chairs. It comes in more than 30 different versions: with and without armrests, in plastic or with a padded seat, with wooden legs, steel legs or castors. It also comes in a whole palette of colours. The chair meets many different needs, whether in the kitchen, the office, the café or the canteen – a true chameleon, disguised as a chair.

About A Chair was nearly rejected before it had a chance to prove itself. Once Welling had designed the chair, he had to make a physical model, a so-called prototype, to show at furniture fairs and sell it to a manufacturer. Only, the company that made the prototype had not followed Welling's drawings but relied on their own ideas and imagination when they made the prototype, so it looked all wrong, and no one wanted to buy it. Fortunately, he was later able to find another manufacturer, who made the chair exactly the way it was drawn.

Welling's idea of using himself and his own ideas about what he wanted from a good chair in the design process proved to be a good approach. About A Chair has become a huge success.

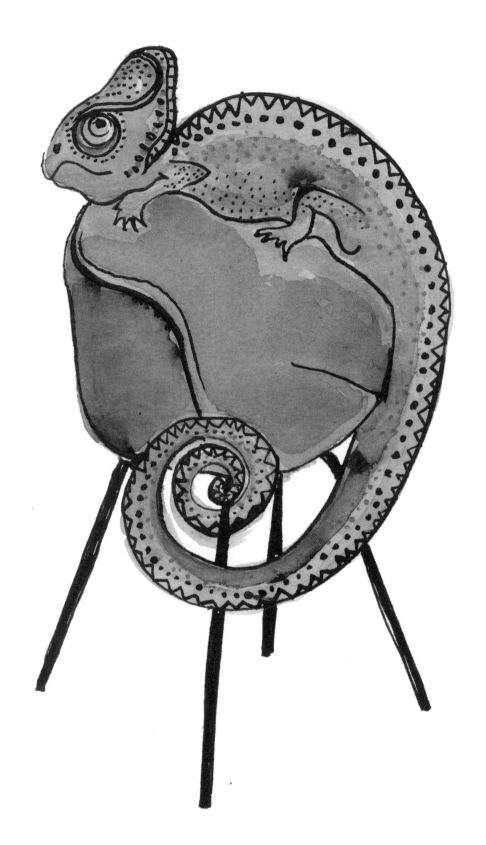

Carlsberg Pilsner label ·
Thorvald Bindesbøll, 1904, and Bo Linnemann, 2011

Leafy lettering

Maybe it is a little cheeky to include a beer label in a book for children, but since it is such a classic graphic design from Denmark, hopefully it will be okay.

In 1904, Carlsberg was appointed a 'Purveyor to the Royal Danish Court', which means that the royal family liked the beer from Carlsberg. To show off the brewery's new status, Carlsberg needed a new label for its Pilsner beer that included a royal crown. The new label was created by designer and architect Thorvald Bindesbøll. He was inspired by the decorative style art nouveau, a style with curvy, organic lines inspired by nature.

When he designed the lettering for the Carlsberg Pilsner label, Bindesbøll was inspired by the hop plant, which delivers one of the key ingredients in beer. The flavour and aroma of beer is balanced by hops, just as the tiny hop leaf above the 'r' visually balances the writing on the label. Hop plants twist and turn when they grow, and this is reflected in the letters. The upper-case 'C' and the final letter, 'g', are parti-

cularly characteristic. With white lettering on a green background topped by a red royal crown, the writing soon came to be the general Carlsberg logo.

In 2011, the logo was carefully renewed by graphic designer Bo Linnemann, who also designed a new typeface for Carlsberg. Linnemann based his work on the original design but simplified both the logo and the lettering. All the letters have soft, rounded forms inspired by the hop plant, and they have little 'feet', just like the main text in this book. These feet are also called serifs. They are the tiny lines at the base of the letters that tie them together and make them easier to read.

If you go into a supermarket and see a Carlsberg beer, the label will look almost the same as the label that was designed more than 100 years ago. So even though the content is freshly brewed, the Carlsberg Pilsner label is a design with an extremely long shelf life.

Georg · Chris L. Halstrøm, 2012

Do touch

Georg is the name of a tow-haired boy, who lives in Copenhagen. But it is also the name of a stool designed by Georg's mother, Chris L. Halstrøm, in 2012. While she was designing the stool, Georg was often with her in the workshop, so she named it after him. It must be fun to eat breakfast sitting on a stool that is named after you.

A stool is a chair without a backrest, a small piece of furniture that fits in just about anywhere. Georg has four legs and is made of ash wood. A wool cushion is tied to the seat with a leather cord. The cushion is a little longer than the seat is wide and seems to invite you to touch it. If you remove the cushion you can use it to stand on if you need to reach something on a high shelf. You can also use it as a small table.

Halstrøm likes to spark our curiosity and wants to make us want to reach out and touch the products she designs. She thinks that using our senses to experience things is important and may help to make our lives richer. Therefore, she has designed Georg out of three natural materials: wool, wood and leather – all materials that are pleasant to touch. All the parts of the stool are visible, and the construction is an important aspect of the design. The stool is an example of Scandinavian minimalism with simplicity and a focus on details as key qualities.

Even if you do not have a mother who is a furniture designer, you probably have a favourite chair at home – if you do, why not name it after yourself?

It remains to be seen whether Georg is a stool that we are going to remember 50 years from now. Still, it is fun to think about the fact that in 50 years' time, Georg is going to be an adult, and he may have children who are the same age Georg is now.

Beoplay A2 · Cecilie Manz, 2014

Sound in motion

In the past, loudspeakers were large furniture items that stood on the floor of the living room, connected by cables to a stereo. They were often big, clunky, ugly boxes, and many families had lengthy negotiations about where to place them. Thankfully, those days are gone! Now we can have small portable speakers that we connect wirelessly to our phones and which we can take with us on the go.

The way we live is reflected in the design we put in our homes. Beoplay A2, which Cecilie Manz designed for Bang & Olufsen, is a loudspeaker for people who are often on the go.

Today, we like to take parts of our home with us when we go out. We eat on the train, drink coffee in the car and listen to music on our way to work or school. We want to be able to take our music with us into the garden, to the bathroom and on a bicycle ride. That is

why Beoplay A2 is designed to be carried like a handbag and hung on a door handle or the handlebars of a bicycle.

During the design process for Beoplay A2, Manz built many different models in polystyrene foam to see whether the form looked nice and to test whether there was room to fit the technical components inside. Models are an important part of the design process – you just cannot figure everything out in your head or on the sketchpad. Afterwards she designed the rest. A collection of delicate old thimbles gave her the idea for the screens. The tiny holes produce a light, lively pattern that lets the sound out on both sides of the speaker.

I wonder what music Manz was listening to when she designed the speaker.

Fold Unfold Fly ·
Margrethe Odgaard, 2015

Setting your table on the fly

When we have dinner guests we often like to decorate the table specially. But … when we unfold the tablecloth it often looks a little tired after being folded up in a cupboard or a drawer.

Textile designer Margrethe Odgaard was unhappy about these folds so she came up with a solution. She designed a tablecloth where the creases are a poetic and humorous part of the design.

Fold Unfold Fly is a plain white tablecloth with colour printed where one would normally fold the tablecloth. The idea is to have the colours highlight the creases. The grey shades that naturally occur in the creases combine with the glow of the colours, making it hard to see where the colour begins and the crease ends.

This draws attention to the creases in the tablecloth, which is something you would normally want to hide. So, in her design, Odgaard turns one of the little practical problems of everyday life into an advantage.

'Fold Unfold' refers to the process the tablecloth undergoes on its journey into the cupboard or the drawer and then back on the table. 'Fly' refers to the coloured print on the tablecloth, which is as light as the touch of a butterfly's wings and almost makes the tablecloth look as if it might take off from the table any moment. And it certainly lets you set the table on the fly, because you do not need to iron the tablecloth to get rid of the creases.

If you want to see Danish design

There are many places in Denmark where you can see and learn more about Danish design.

Museums and galleries:

A. Petersen
Kløvermarksvej 70
2300 Copenhagen S

Brandts
Brandts Torv 1
5000 Odense C

Clay – Museum of Ceramic Art Denmark
Kongebrovej 42
5500 Middelfart

Dansk Møbelkunst Gallery
Aldersrogade 6C
2100 Copenhagen Ø

Designmuseum Danmark
Bredgade 68
1260 Copenhagen K

Etage Projects
Borgergade 15E
1300 Copenhagen K

Finn Juhl's house
Kratvænget 15
2920 Charlottenlund

Glasmuseet Ebeltoft
Strandvejen 8
8400 Ebeltoft

Klassik
Bredgade 3
1260 Copenhagen K

Louisiana Museum of Modern Art
Gammel Strandvej 13
3050 Humlebæk

Officinet – Danish Crafts & Design Association's Project Space
Bredgade 66
1260 Copenhagen K

Trapholt – Museum of Modern Art And Design
Æblehaven 23
6000 Kolding

Wegner Museum
Wegner Plads 1
6270 Tønder

The Royal Danish Academy of Fine Arts, School of Design and Design School Kolding often have exhibitions showing the latest examples of Danish design, so the two schools may also be interesting places to visit:

Royal Danish Academy of Fine Arts, School of Design
Philip De Langes Allé 10
1435 Copenhagen K

Design School Kolding
Ågade 10
6000 Kolding

And of course, there are lots of shops where you can see and try out many of the things and pieces of furniture included in the book.

When you visit family and friends, you can also see if you can find some of the design objects you have read about in this book.

Glossary – key terms and concepts

Here is a list of some of the special terms that are used in this book with an explanation of what the terms mean in connection with design.

Aesthetic

The word 'aesthetic' comes from Greek and means something we sense. Aesthetic is a philosophical concept that is often used in connection with art and beauty. In design, we use the word 'aesthetic' to describe something we think is particularly good or beautiful. For example, we might say that a chair has aesthetic qualities, or that it is an aesthetic pleasure to drink from a particular cup. The way we use 'aesthetic' today, it is not only about how something looks but also, for example, how it feels. The full sensory experience.

Bauhaus

Bauhaus was a German school of design, art and architecture that was founded in 1919 and closed in 1933. The school wanted to combine art and craft in a new way. Bauhaus focused on functionalism and became known for a new design expression or look that avoided unnecessary decoration in order to highlight the beauty of the form itself. This expression often included clear geometric shapes like cubes, cylinders and balls and typically used new industrial materials, such as steel and glass.

Copy

Basically, a copy means something that is exactly the same as something else. Often there is one original and a number of copies. In design, some copies are illegal because someone reproduced a product without getting the original designer's permission.

Craft, craftsmanship

Good craftsmanship is the key to quality craft products – for example, carefully crafted wood, ceramics or knitwear. Craft objects are usually one-off or unique products because they are handmade, unlike design, which is often mass-produced. Still, a crafts maker can make a series of objects that are almost identical, for example matching ceramic cups.

The Danish Design School, School of Arts and Crafts

Over the years, the name has varied. Today, the school where many Danish designers trained is called the Royal Danish Academy of Fine Arts, Schools of Architecture, Design and Conservation. Because the name is so long, many simply call it by the Danish abbreviation KADK. The school was founded in 1875 and is now located on the small island of Holmen in Copenhagen.

Form follows function

An important principle in architecture and industrial design in the 20th century. It means letting the function of an object decide its form and its expression (look).

Functionalism

A style that developed during the 20th century. Functionalism means letting the function of an object (how it will work) decide its form and expression (look). The functionalists also aimed for a form that could be mass-produced. This meant moving away from handmade products and a very decorative look and instead going for a simpler, cleaner, more streamlined form with no superfluous elements.

Furniture designer

Someone who designs furniture. A furniture designer may be trained as a designer, an architect, a cabinetmaker or a carpenter, or he or she may simply have a talent for making furniture. It is not a protected title, so in principle anyone who wants to can claim to be a furniture designer.

Golden age of Danish design

The period of 1945–75 is often called the golden age of Danish design. During this time, Danish furniture design in particular flourished, and this made Denmark well known throughout the world. Many of the important Danish furniture classics were created during this period.

Icon

An icon originally meant a religious image – for example, an image of Jesus Christ or the Virgin Mary. However, when the term is used in connection with design, it has nothing to do with religion. Here it is used about objects that have special status. They have become classics that many people know or recognize.

Laminate

Laminate is a material that can be used to make furniture. It is made of many layers of paper mixed with resin. Under intense heat, the mass is compressed into a board that looks somewhat similar to wood but is much cheaper.

Less is more

A concept articulated by the German architect Mies van der Rohe. The point is that keeping things simple is the key to good design. Minimalism is based on the concept of 'less is more' and aims for simple, pared-down designs based on straight lines and, in many cases, clean geometric shapes.

Manufacturer

A manufacturer is the company that puts a design into production in cooperation with the designer. Sometimes, the designer contacts a manufacturer to see if they would be interested in putting a new design into production. Sometimes, the manufacturer contacts a designer to ask him or her to design a particular product. There are many design manufacturers in Denmark, including Fritz Hansen, Holmegaard, Royal Copenhagen and Hay.

Minimalism

Minimalism is about focusing on what is most important and leaving out the rest. Minimalist designers aim for simple forms, materials and colours and limit the presence of details or decorative elements. Some see minimalism as a clean and honest style; others find it boring. Everyone has their own taste.

Organic form/design expression

A look that finds inspiration in the world of nature and prefers soft, rounded, natural shapes over straight lines and sharp angles. Verner Panton and Nanna Ditzel are some of the best-known Danish representatives of organic design.

Patent

If someone has a patent on something, it means that he or she is the only person in the world who is legally permitted to make this one particular thing. A patent protects the design from being copied by others. To get a patent you have to apply for it, and you have to be able to prove that you were the first person ever to make that particular product. It is a good idea to apply for a patent if you invent something new because it protects your legal rights to the invention.

Plywood

A material that is often used to make furniture. It is made of very thin layers of wood that are placed on top of each other in criss-cross layers and glued together. The result is a board that is both stronger and more flexible than a board made of solid wood.

Proportions

Proportions are about relative size – for example, the size of a chair's seat, back and legs in relation to each other and the size of the chair in relation to the human body. The size and proportions of a product are often designed to match the body. For example, a glass that is too big for our hands is difficult to drink from. In 1948, the Swiss architect Le Corbusier developed a system called Modulor based on the proportions of the human body, which many designers and architects still use today.

Prototype

When a designer is preparing to put a design object into production, he or she first makes a prototype, often in cooperation with the manufacturer. A prototype can also be called a test model. It is expensive to put things into production, so it is a good idea to test the use, quality, size and look of the new product before making a big investment. Often, the design process includes several prototypes before the final model is ready.

Scale

Scale is an important concept in design. A model or prototype of a product is often made in a scale of 1:10. This means that the model is 10 times smaller than the actual product is going to be. A scale model gives a sense of whether the shapes and proportions look right and are harmonious.

Shell chair

A chair type where the back and the seat consist of a shell – that is, a single piece of wood or plastic that has been bent or moulded into the right shape. The shell is mounted on an undercarriage or frame, which forms the legs or the base of the chair.

Upholstery

Fabric or leather that is used to cover a piece of furniture, like a chair or a sofa. Often, there is padding in the form of foam rubber or some other soft material underneath the upholstery to make the furniture more comfortable.

Your own pages

Here you can draw some of the design objects you think are missing in the book:

The Little Book of Danish Design for Children and Curious Grown-Ups

First edition, second print run
ISBN: 978-87-93604-56-8

Cover design and layout:
Søren Damstedt, Trefold
Illustrations: Kitt Stuart Schwenn
Consultant: Pernille Stockmarr
Editing: Sidsel Kjærulff Rasmussen
Translation: Dorte Herholdt Silver
Proofreading: Wendy Brouwer
The book is set in Replica and Chronicle Text
Paper: Munken Lynx Rough 150 g
Pre-press: Narayana Press, Gylling
Printing and binding: Jelgavas Tipogrāfija
Printed in Latvia 2023

Strandberg Publishing A/S
Gammel Mønt 14
1117 Copenhagen K
Denmark
www.strandbergpublishing.dk

The original Danish version was
published with support from the
following private foundations:

Beckett-Fonden
Nikolai og Felix Fonden
New Carlsberg Foundation
POLITIKEN-FONDEN